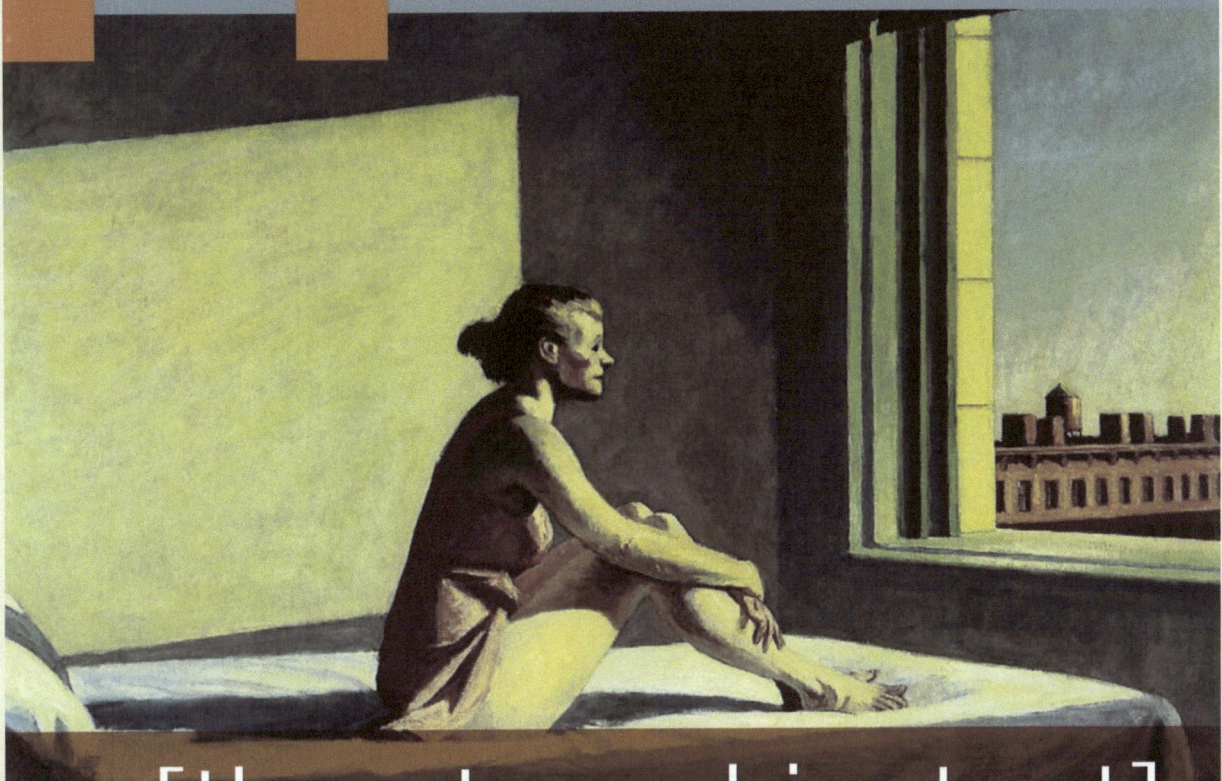

edward hopper
[the eternal instant]

edited by
Elena Pontiggia

with the participation of
Paola Bacuzzi,
Silvia Banzatti,
Andrea Bonalume,
Gabriele Cantoni,
Camillo Fornasieri,
Miriam Melzi,
Marco Vianello

video editing
Romina Ronchi

graphics
Sabrina Toni

production managers
Maria Edwige Angelini,
Elisa Bolognesi,
Elena Desco,
Angelo Matteoni,
Marco Migani

coordinating manager
Maurizio Bellucci

set-up team
Gemma Faberi,
Stefania Colini,
Marta Stacchini

printing
Millennium

exhibit rental
I.E.S. (International Exhibition Service)
www.meetingmostre.com

thanks to
Roberto Buggio
Art Center
Bernareggio (MI)

English translation
Bruno Cassarà
Joshua Stancil

© English Translation:
Revolution of Tenderness
ISBN-13: 978-1727420173
ISBN-10: 1727420179

rimini meeting 2006

Exhibit created and organized by the Meeting for Friendship Among Peoples on the occasion of its 27th edition

English translation created for use in the United States of America by Revolution of Tenderness on the occasion of the sixth edition of the Festival of Friendship in Pittsburgh

[the eternal instant]

Largely forgotten in the decades immediately following his death, with the era's art history textbooks granting him scant mention, Edward Hopper (Nyack 1882—New York 1967) is today considered the greatest American painter of the twentieth century. His works, as many have come to recognize, depict and reflect on the contemporary world.

Hopper was a realist painter. In his art an America takes form that is both modern and intriguingly traditional: no skyscrapers or cars, but rather train tracks, colonial houses with white wood and triangular roofs, Victorian mansards with chimneys, and lighthouses on the Atlantic coast.

It is an America represented in her common places: gas stations, cafés, drugstores, shops, apartments, and hotel rooms, peopled by figures aware of their own solitude.

Nevertheless, into this everyday reality sneaks the intuition of a further dimension: a "beyond" that is greater and more mysterious than the impressions given at first sight. When time stands still (and in depicting this stillness, Hopper is a follower of De Chirico's metaphysical style), daily life reveals all its complexity.

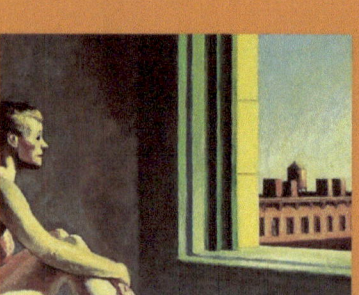

Hopper was a passionate reader of Emerson, the great American philosopher of the nineteenth century.

"The foundations of man are not in matter, but in spirit. And the element of spirit is eternity," wrote Emerson.

In Hopper's paintings, too, where time stands still and all is bathed in an unblinking light, there emerges a search for the eternal.

Certainly, his works (which draw on modern European art even as they witness to the need to find his American roots, thereby participating in the dialogue with tradition) express dramatically man's loneliness in the contemporary world. And yet, just as in Verlaine's poem, "The Exquisite Hour," which Hopper particularly loved, they also reveal a sort of **"eternal instant"** in which, behind varied and ever-changing appearances, transpires an intimation of the infinite.

Light is the foremost element in all of Hopper's works. In his final paintings, he presents figures who, wherever they are, desperately seek the light of the sun. Yet light is not merely an atmospheric phenomenon, but a dimension that is at once realistic and transcendent, physical and metaphysical.

biography

1882: Edward Hopper is born on July 22nd in Nyack, just a few miles from New York City. He is the son of Garrett Henry Hopper and Elisabeth Griffiths Smith, niece to the founder of the local Baptist church.

1899-1900: After his high school graduation, and pressured by his parents, he studies at New York's Correspondence School of Illustrating. He does eventually become an illustrator, but the work never truly interests him.

1900-1905: He studies at the New York School of Art. First illustration, then painting with William Chase, Kenneth Miller, and, most importantly, Robert Henri.

1906-1907: Having graduated, he begins work as an illustrator. He goes to Paris, where he studies the Impressionist painters. He travels throughout Europe, visiting London, Amsterdam, and Berlin.

1908: Once back in New York, he becomes part of a collective with Henry's other students. Hopper is the only one whose works are not inspired by New York City life, depicting instead everyday Parisian scenes.

1909: He travels to Paris again.

1910: He participates in a second collective. He travels to Europe a third time (Paris and Spain). His return to the United States is for him the beginning of a crisis.

1912: He paints in Gloucester, Massachusetts, and then in Ogunquit, Maine.

1913: Opening of the Armory Show, the first exhibit in the United States to feature the European avant-garde. Hopper presents a single work, Sailing, his first to be sold.

1915: He devotes himself to etching, a technique he will use in some sixty works.

1920: His first personal exhibit at the Whitney Studio Club.

1923: He begins working with watercolors.

1924: His first personal watercolor exhibit, which portrays American subjects. It represents a definitive commitment to art and the abandonment of illustration. He marries Josephine Verstille Nivison.

1927: Another exhibit with oil paintings, watercolors, and prints at the Rehn Gallery.

1930: He goes to Cape Cod for the first time. It will become his summer home for the rest of his life.

1933: His first retrospective at the Museum of Modern Art in New York. He builds his home in Cape Cod. He travels to Canada and Maine.

1934: He travels to Colorado, Utah, Nevada, California, Oregon, and Wyoming.

1935-1946: He is awarded numerous prizes and acknowledgments; he travels to Mexico four times.

1950: Retrospective at the Whitney Museum of American Art, the Museum of Fine Arts in Boston, and at the Detroit Institute of Art.

1952: He is nominated as one of four American representatives at the Venice Biennial.

1953-1966: He continues to gather fame in grand retrospectives and important exhibits.

1967: Represents the United States at the San Paolo Biennial. He dies on May 15th in his New York studio. His wife, Jo, dies less than a year later.

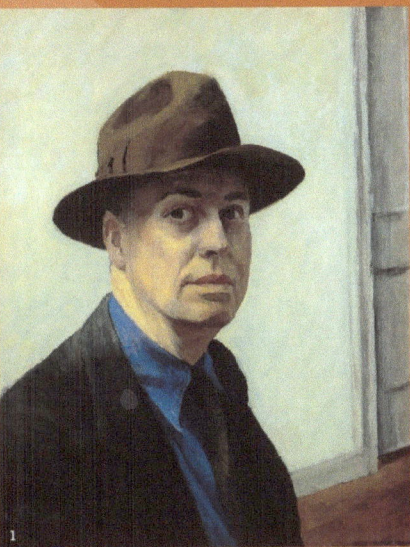
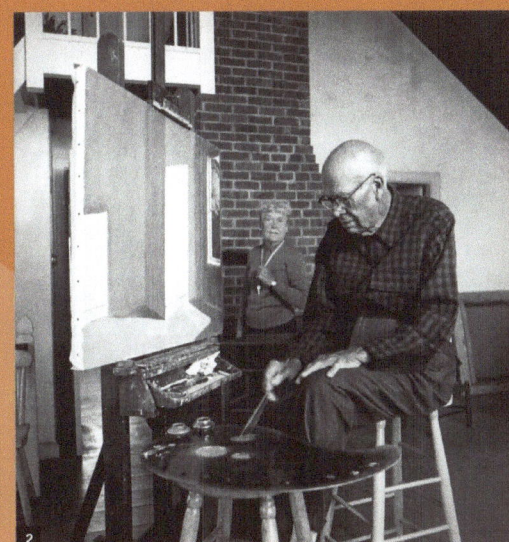

1. *Self Portrait*, 1925-30
oil on canvas, 64.1x52.4 cm
New York, The Whitney Museum of American Art

2. *Hopper in His Studio*

"In the artist's first works lies already the seed of a future search. The artist builds his work around himself, his personality, which changes little from his birth to his death. The artist continues to be that which he already was."
(Hopper, 1935)

training

In 1900, the eighteen-year-old Hopper attends New York's Chase School, an art institute where Merritt Chase and Robert Henri both teach. His first works are characterized by those dense and dark hues that Henri preferred. In the artist's portraits and self-portraits, the figures in the foreground emerge bathed in light, in contrast with the black background—an inspiration drawn from Rembrandt but also from Manet.

Tradition and modernity are not here contraposed because, as Hopper states, artists "remain forever modern by the fundamental truth that is in them. It makes Molière at his greatest as new as Ibsen, or Giotto as modern as Cézanne" (Hopper, 1933).

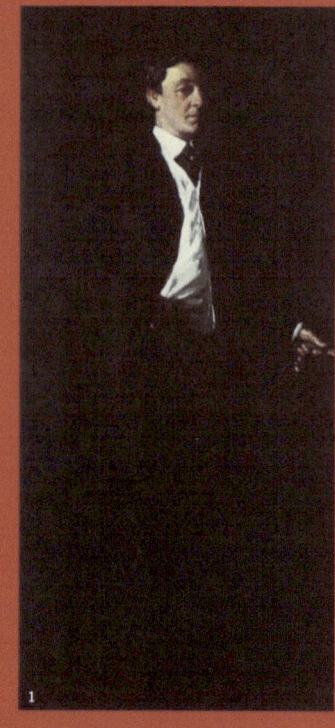

1. **Robert Henri,**
Portrait of William Glackens, 1904
oil on canvas, 198x96.5 cm
Lincoln, The Nebraska Art Association

2. ***Painter and Model***, 1902-04
oil on cardboard, 26x20.5 cm
New York, Whitney Museum of American Art

3. ***Self Portrait***, 1903-06
oil on canvas, 65.9x55.9 cm
New York, Whitney Museum of American Art

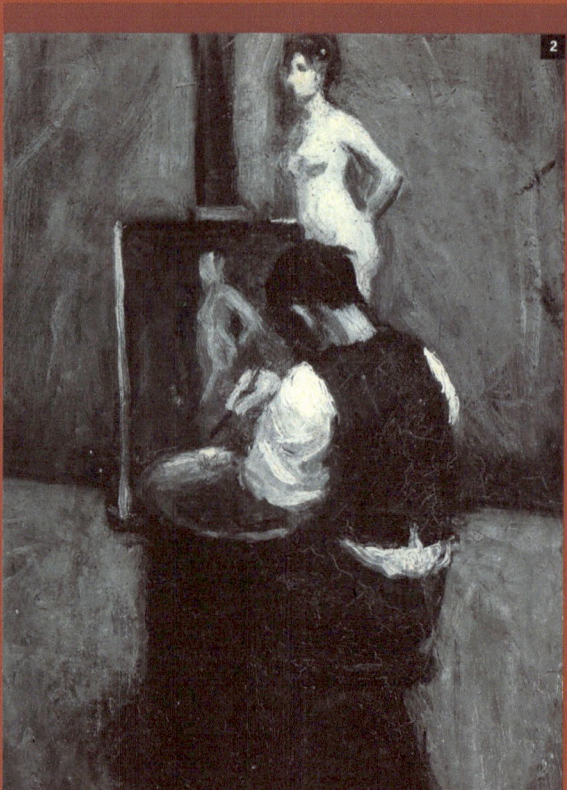
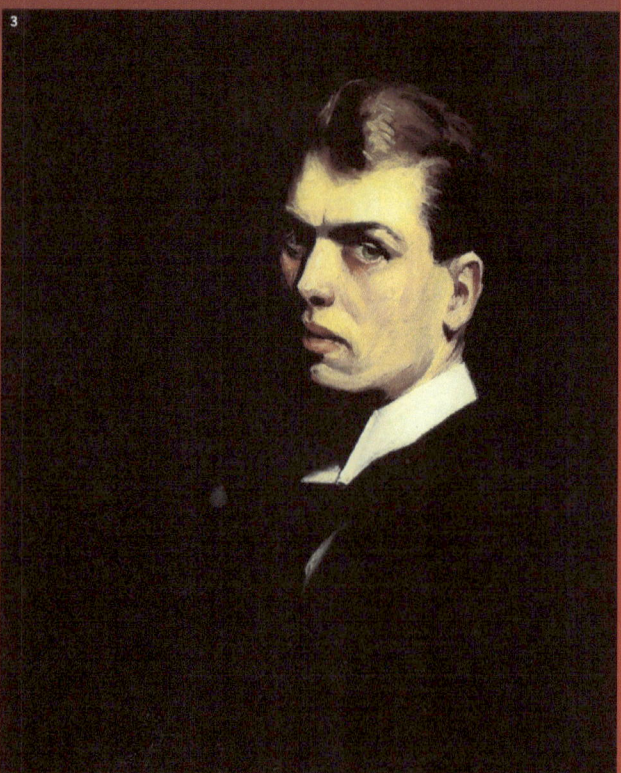

According to Henri, "Mediocre art limits itself to saying that it is night. True art, on the other hand, gives the feeling of the night. It is closer to reality, while the former is only a copy." Hopper learns from him to combine observation and expression.

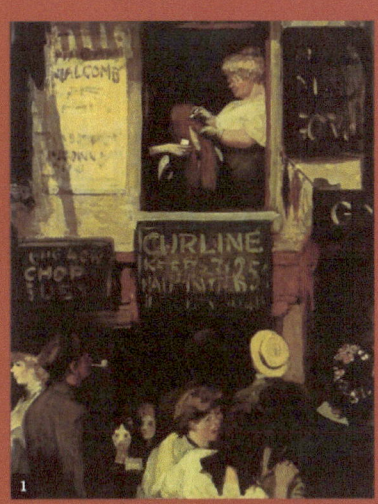

the group of eight

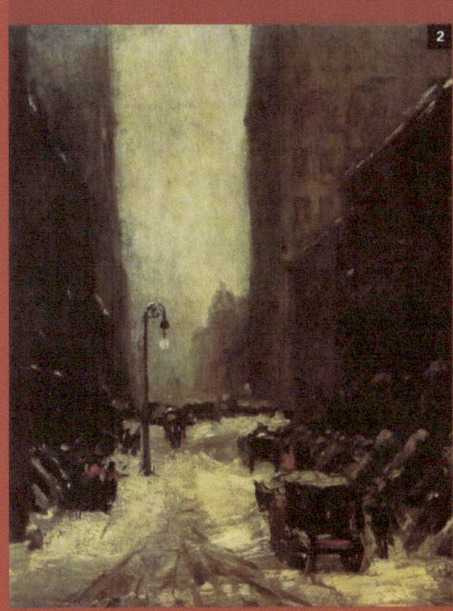
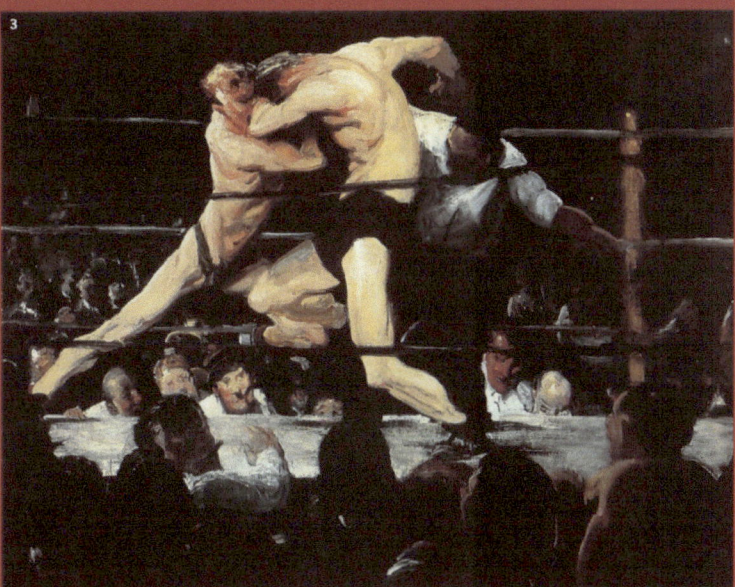

"The Eight," a group of painters comprising the likes of Henri, Sloan, Lucks, and others, rises to prominence and scandalizes the American art scene. Realist in their inspiration, these artists portray American city life, drawing on Manet and French realism.

Though their works are not particularly crude, nevertheless their realism shocks—so much so that the group is renamed (somewhat cruelly) the "Ashcan School."

From Henri and these others, Hopper learns to always keep his art in relation to life, thus rejecting subjects from literature, history, mythology, and religion, and concentrating instead on the reality of the everyday.

1. **John Sloan,**
Hairdresser's window, 1907
oil on canvas, 81x66 cm
Hartford, Wadsworth Athenaeum

2. **Robert Henri,**
Snow in New York, 1902
oil on canvas, 81.5x65.3 cm
Washington, National Gallery of Art

3. **George Bellows,**
Stag at Sharkey's, 1909
oil on canvas, 99x122.6 cm
Cleveland, The Cleveland Museum of Art

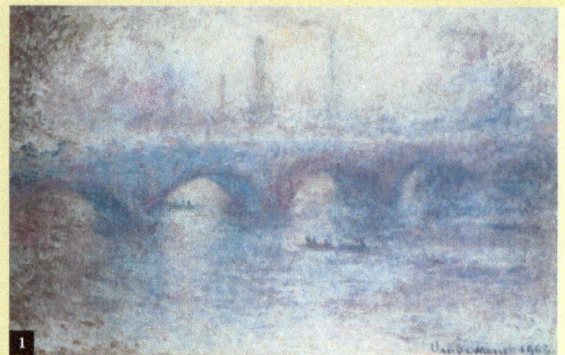

the journey to paris

"Hopper's light is the opposite of Monet's, which dematerializes everything. Monet transforms the sturdy stone of the Waterloo Bridge into a blue-violet spot on the canvas. Hopper, instead, paints his memory of the objects, which is more solid than the memories of light and air."
(Mark Strand).

Spurred by his love for Rembrandt, Goya, Manet, Degas, and Renoir, Hopper travels to Paris in 1906. The discovery of the French capital is thrilling: "I liked the city's physiognomy. I painted alone, in the streets, along the river, and had the Impressionists in mind. But theirs was not a lasting influence. What I really learned was to brighten my tones." In fact, in Paris Hopper discovers light and brighter colors even as he remains original in the choice of subject matter. He does not care particularly for the water, skies, flowers, and gardens traditionally taken up in Impressionist painting. He prefers themes that give a sense of lasting solidity to the emotion of the fleeting moment.

1. **Claude Monet,**
Waterloo Bridge. Effect of Fog, 1903
oil on canvas, 50x65 cm
St. Petersburg, Ermitage

2. *Bistro,* 1909
oil on canvas, 59.4x72.4 cm
New York, Whitney Museum of American Art

3. *Steps in Paris,* 1906
oil on panel, 33x23.3 cm
New York, Whitney Museum of American Art

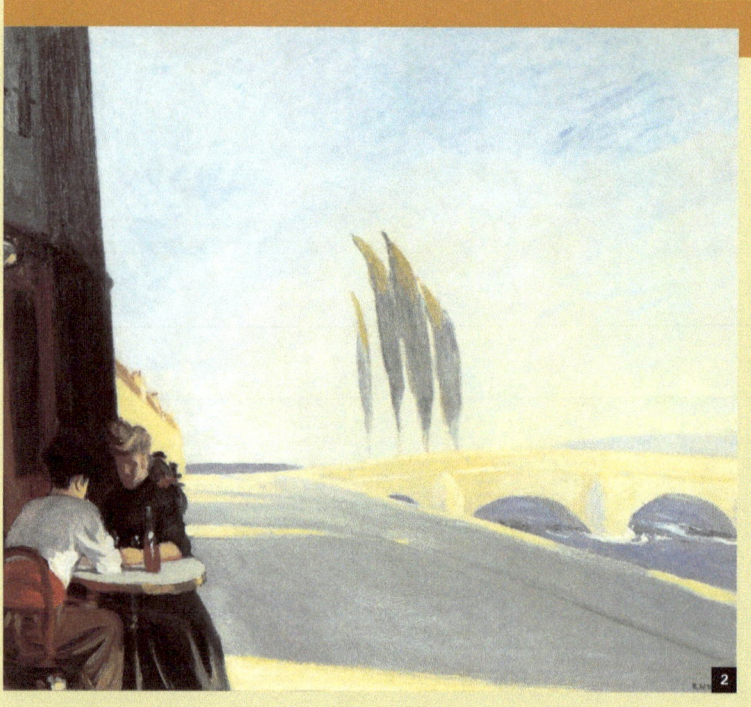

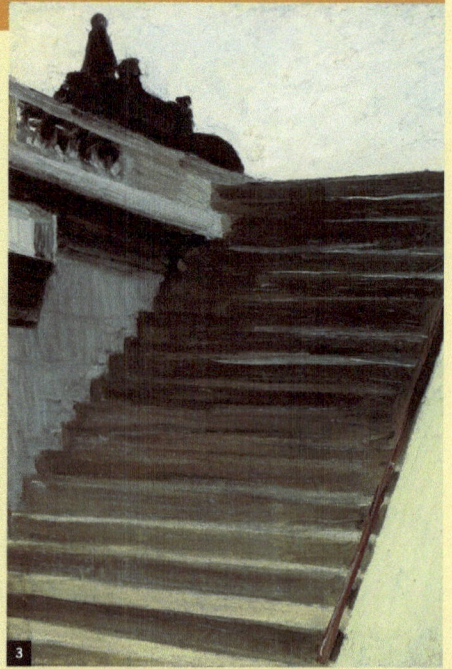

In Paris, "The light was different from anything I had known. The shadows were luminous, more [things] reflected light. Even under the bridges there was a certain luminosity" (Hopper, 1956).
Hopper's light, however, is the opposite of the impressionists': it does not separate the various elements, but rather preserves their shape and structure.

1. **Le Pont des Arts**, 1907
oil on canvas, 58.6x71.3 cm
New York, Whitney Museum of American Art

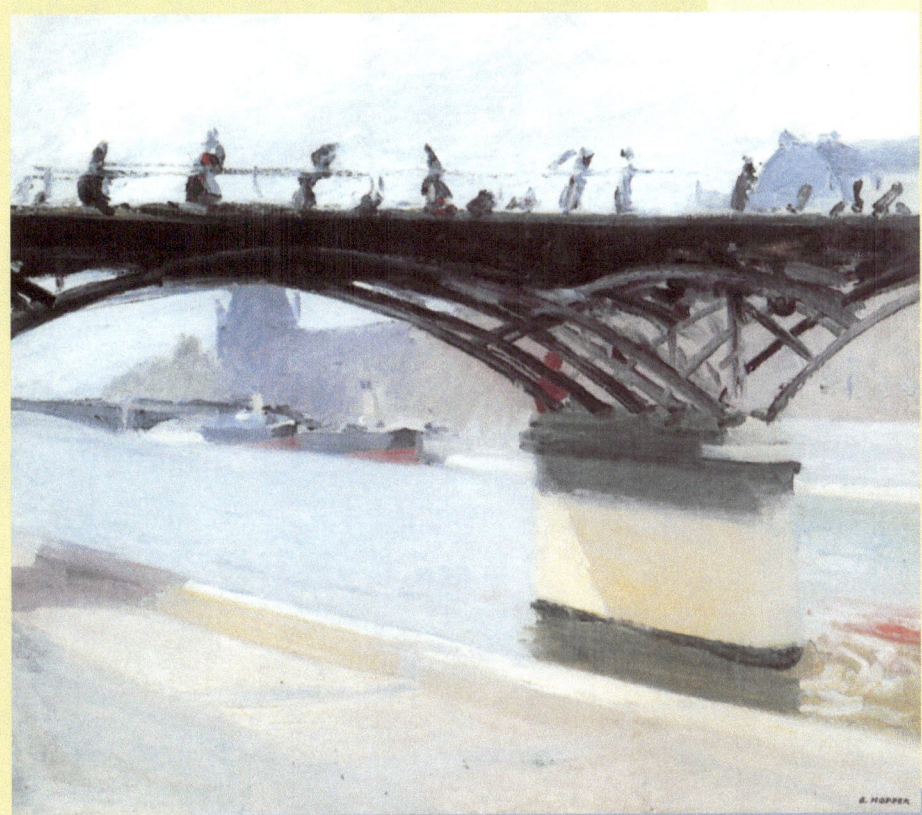

Each figure appears as if acting in a play: the ruffian, the woman with heavy makeup, the pierrot, the elegant couple. An apparent calm pervades the establishment, which resembles the typical Parisian café. The depiction of men as actors, which is also emphasized by the brightness of color learned from the Fauves, is a metaphor for life: under the appearances and roles that modern society forces upon us, we are left with a melancholic aftertaste because pretending cannot eliminate the demand for meaning that characterizes the human heart.

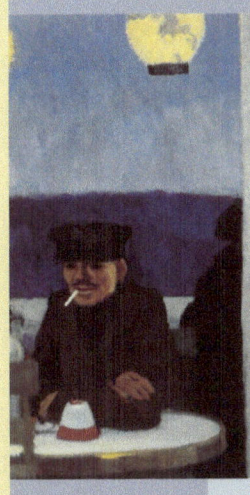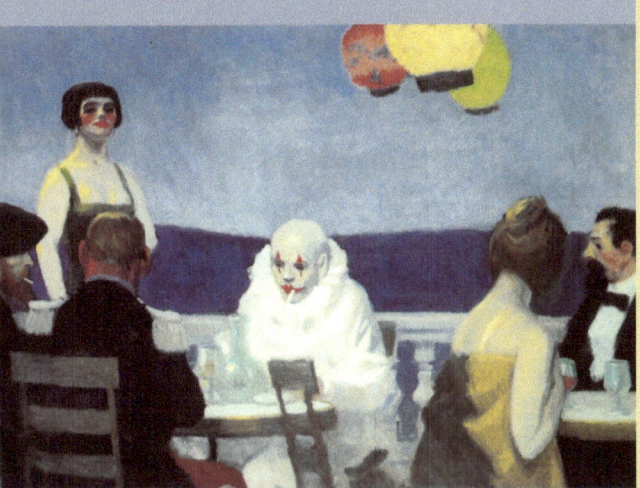

1. **Soir Bleu**, 1914
oil on canvas, 91.4x182.9 cm
New York, Whitney Museum of American Art

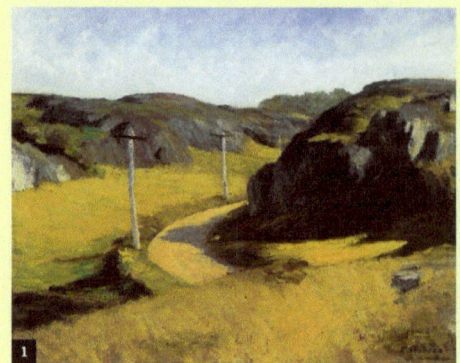

return to america

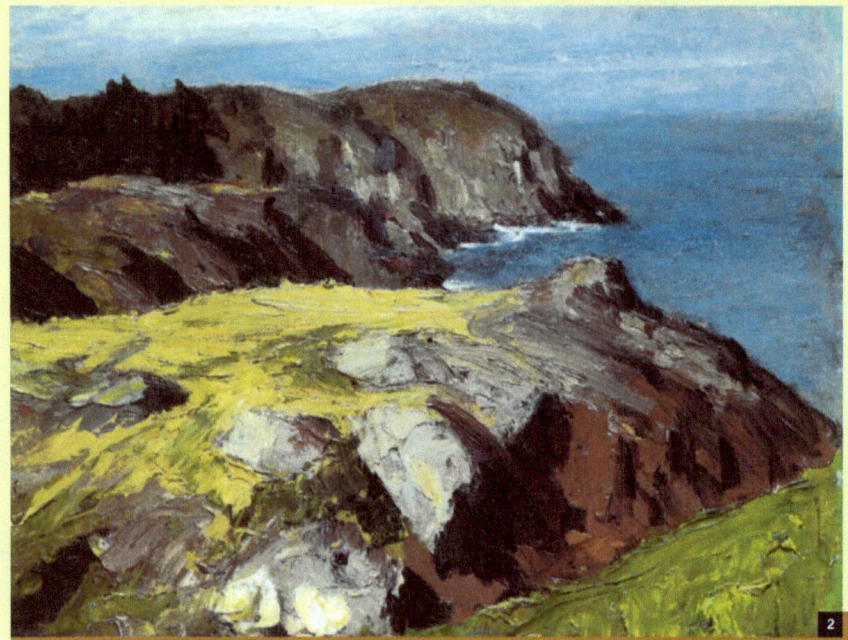

"It seemed awful crude and raw here when I got back [to America]. It took me ten years to get over Europe."

1. **Street in Maine**, 1914
oil on canvas, 61x73.7 cm
New York, Whitney Museum of American Art

2. **Blackheard, Monhegan,** 1916-1919
oil on canvas, 24.1x33 cm
New York, Whitney Museum of American Art

Upon his return in 1911, the impact with America plunges Hopper into crisis. In these years he paints pictures that reveal the influence of French culture.
Nevertheless, he reflects on the need to reconnect with his tradition, thus setting aside the imitation of European art: "The domination of France in the...arts has been almost complete for the last thirty years or more in this country. If an apprenticeship to a master has been necessary, I think we have served it. Any further relation of such a character can only mean humiliation to us" (Hopper, 1959).
In 1913, the Armory Show exhibit opens in New York. There, Americans can observe European art closely for the first time. Hopper understands its significance but insists that it is necessary to seek out the peculiarities of American art. "Native particularities are the only ones that interest us, because they are born of the artist's reaction before his own land and are formed and inspired by the heritage of his nationality" (Hopper, 1933).

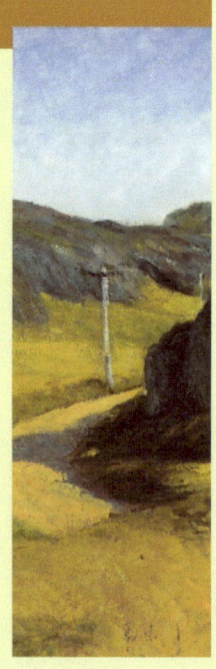

The years between 1911 and 1924 are difficult for the painter. He is not well-known and is unable to support himself with his art. He must therefore work in illustration to survive. Still, even in this field he crafts significant works and develops motifs that he will pick up again later.

illustration

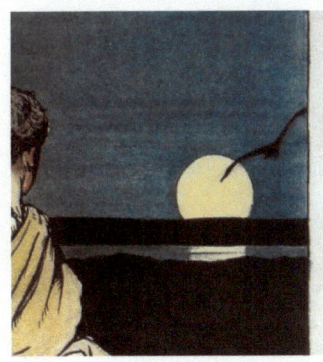

In *Boy and Moon*, he constructs a space that is at once internal and external: the hilly landscape seems to trespass into the boy's room, a device that can also be found in his later, more mature works.

With *In a Restaurant*, Hopper is able to make compelling a banal, everyday circumstance (a simple conversation in a restaurant) by lowering the vantage point, as a film director would. Reality is not just seen but mentally recast.

1. ***Boy and Moon***
watercolor and ink on paper, 55.6x37 cm
New York, Whitney Museum of American Art

2. ***In a Restaurant,*** 1916-25
charcoal on paper, 67.6x55.1 cm
New York, Whitney Museum of American Art

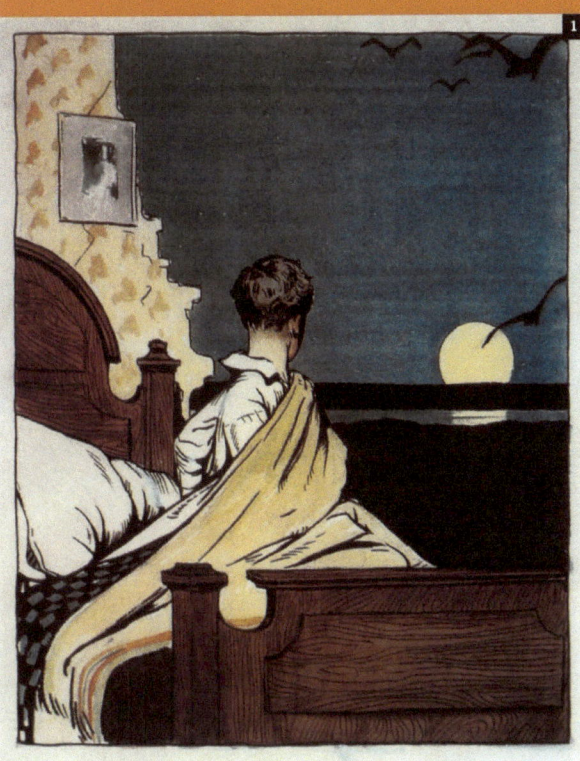
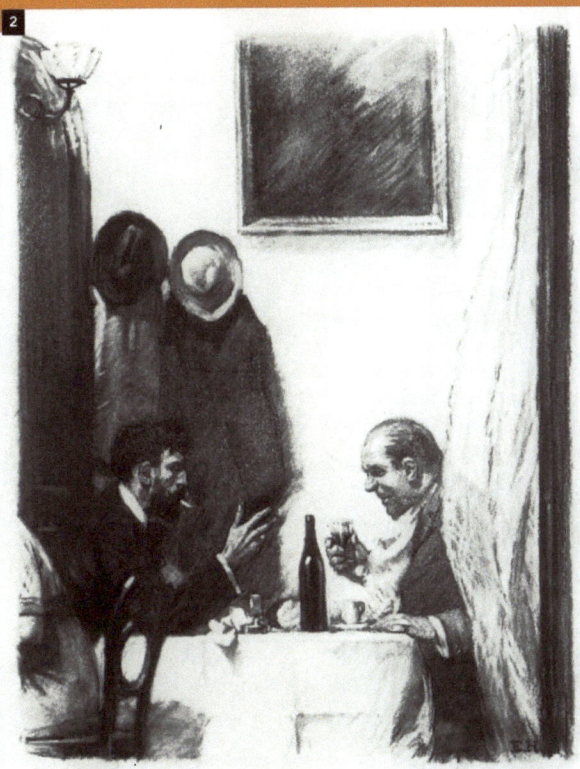

In the early 1920s, Hopper begins etching, revealing the same way of looking at reality.

etching

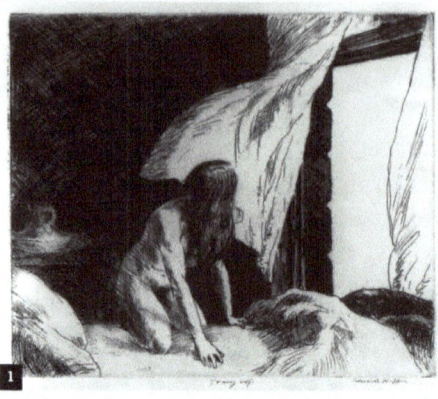

In *Night Shadows*, the scene is observed from above and at an oblique angle. It is a simple scene (a passerby walks alone along the street), but the contrast between the light from the streetlamp and the darkness of the night, a contrast underlined by the long shadows cast on the sidewalk, evokes a subtle sense of mystery.
In *Evening Wind*, the light that enters from the window imbues a woman's body and the wind shakes the curtains. In this ordinary scene, one feels an inexplicable sense of suspense.
The search for the mystery hidden where there seems to be no mystery—precisely this is the heart of Hopper's art.

1. ***Evening Wind***, 1921
etching, 17.5x21 cm
New York, Whitney Museum of American Art

2. ***Night Shadows***, 1921
etching, 17.5x21 cm
New York, Whitney Museum of American Art

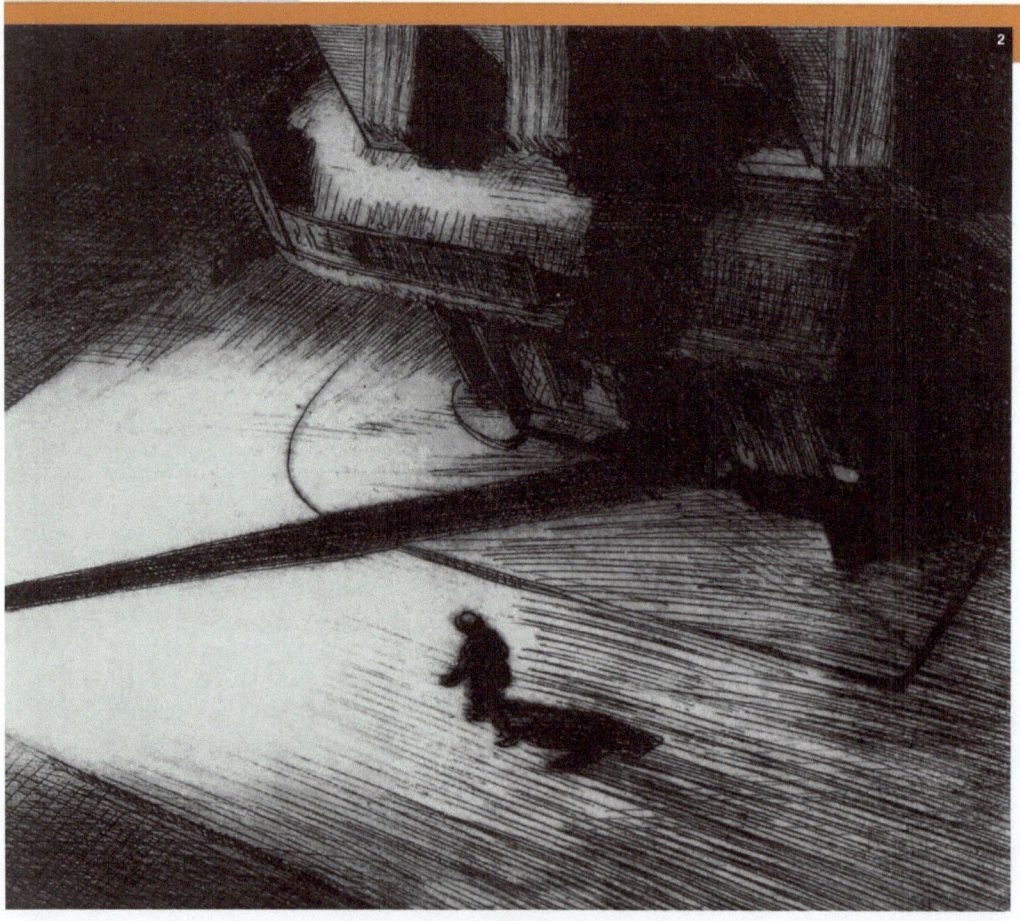

the relationship with de chirico

In the absolute stillness of light, reality seems to hang forever in an eternal instant. When removed from the flow of time, things are no longer ordinary instruments but mysterious signs.

The enigmatic quality of Hopper's paintings is reminiscent of the artworks of De Chirico, the father of "metaphysical" painting: a style that interrogates not the shapes, but the meaning (or lack thereof) of things. More than any clear references to De Chirico's paintings, Hopper's works reflect the Italian painter's influence in their quality of suspended air, in their clear and geometric light, and in their construction of spaces. The art critic Stuart Preston called Hopper the "American De Chirico," while the writer Peter Handke compares the magic in Hopper's paintings to "De Chirico's empty, metaphysical piazzas."

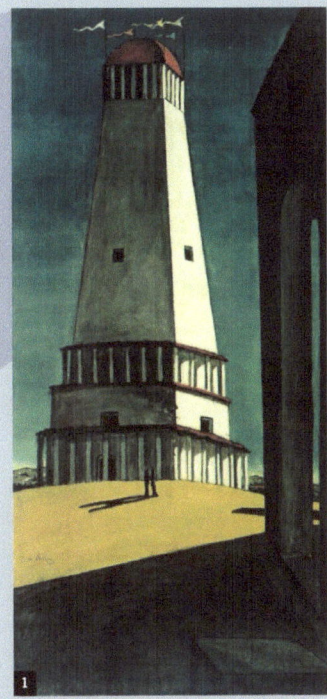

1. **G. De Chirico**,
The Nostalgia of the Infinite, 1913
oil on canvas, 135x64 cm
New York, The Museum of Modern Art

2. **G. De Chirico**,
The Red Tower, 1913
oil on canvas, 74x100 cm
Venezia, Peggy Guggenheim Collection

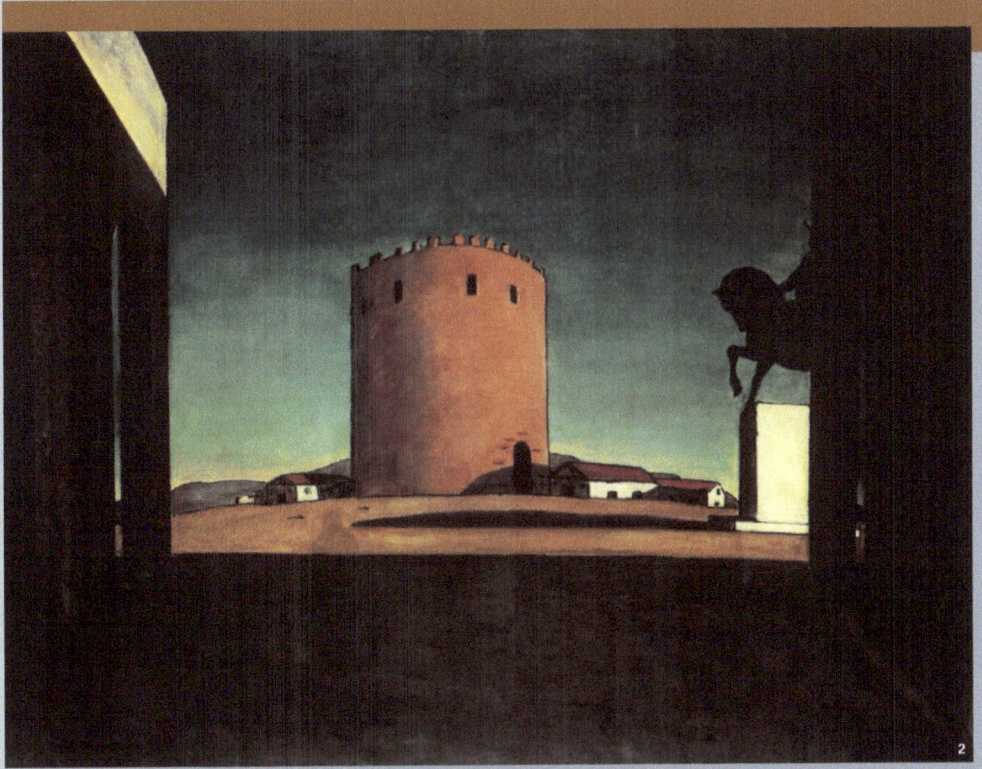

In these years, Hopper spends much of his time painting lighthouses on the ocean's edge – *The Lighthouse at Two Lights*, for example, where the interplay between light and shadow recalls De Chirico's *The Nostalgia of the Infinite*. However, unlike the Italian painter, Hopper includes signs of hope.
While De Chirico often places a sleeping Arianna in the midst of his plazas (in classical mythology, Arianna helps Theseus exit the labyrinth, and her slumber symbolizes the impossibility of finding a way out of it), the purpose of the lighthouse is to light the way, to be a reference point for the sailor.
Often in Hopper's works, everyday objects and settings represent something greater, something that goes beyond what we see immediately.

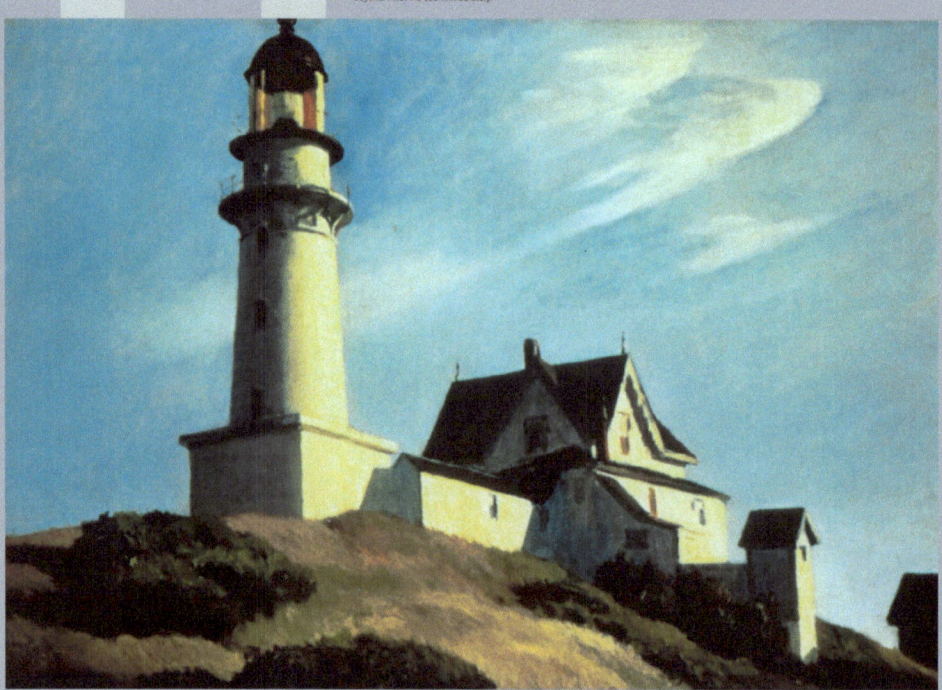

1. *The Lighthouse at Two Lights*, 1929
oil on canvas, 74.9x109.9 cm
New York, The Metropolitan Museum of Art

"No event is so unimportant that it should be curtailed or eliminated just to make room for something more compelling or important" (Wim Wenders).
Wenders himself defines Hopper's paintings as "the beginnings of American film."

hopper and cinema

Hopper's paintings, with their extraordinary power of suggestion, have inspired many directors. In 1954, Hitchcock brings distinctly Hopperian angles to the frames of *Rear Window*; in 1960, *House by the Railroad* provides inspiration for the Bates Motel, the setting for Norman's murders.
In Wim Wenders' films, from *Paris, Texas* (1984) to *The End of Violence* (1998), we see suspensions in the narration that allude to Hopper's paintings as they signal the desire to halt time itself.

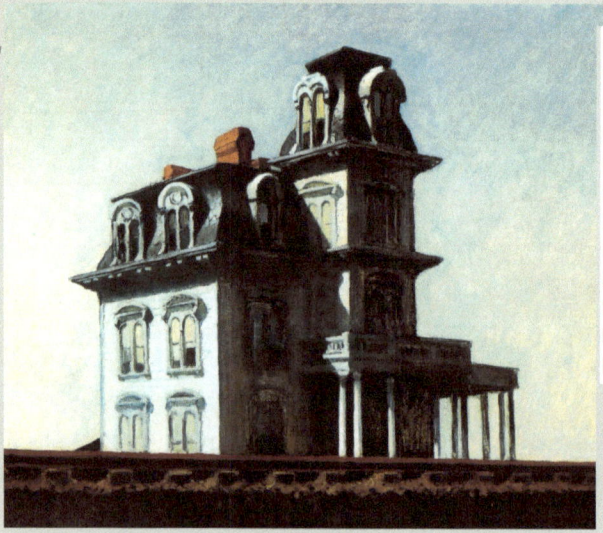

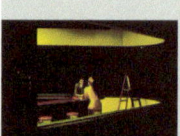
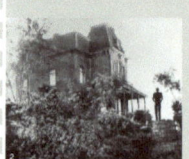

1. *The End of Violence*, 1998
directed by W. Wenders

2. *Psycho*, 1960
directed by A. Hitchcock

3. *House by the Railroad*, 1925
oil on canvas, 60.7x73.7 cm
New York, The Museum of Modern Art

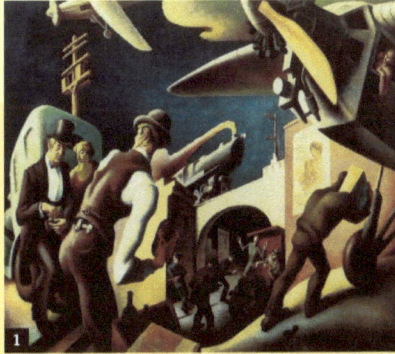

hopper and the american scene

1. **Thomas Hart Benton**
Bootleggers, 1927
oil and tempura on canvas,
168x183.2 cm
Winston-Salem, Reynolda House,
Museum of American Art

2. *New York Movie*, 1939
oil on canvas, 81.9x101.9 cm
New York, The Museum of Modern Art

In the '30s and '40s, Hopper is considered a major figure in the "American Scene," a realist style that seeks to represent life and society in the United States.

The label is inaccurate, however, and Hopper himself disagrees with it. While Thomas Hart Benton, one of the American Scene's major exponents, paints especially the folkloric and historical aspects of America, Hopper seeks to represent more universal and less anecdotal elements, even as he paints places and situations in contemporary New York.

What's more, Hopper works by synthesizing, eliminating as many details as possible. He describes this process as the attempt to conserve the original vision, which is obscured by the addition of unnecessary elements as it is transposed onto the canvas. Simplification of form and essentiality of vision are the fundamental characteristics of Hopper's method.

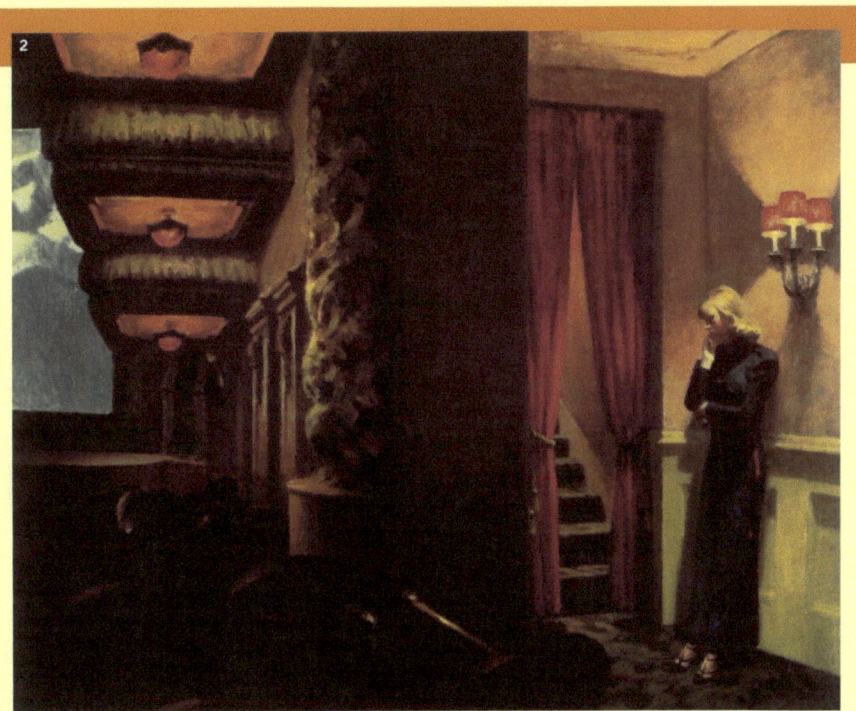

Sitting at his desk, a man is absorbed in his reading. Next to him stands a woman about to open a file cabinet and looking at a paper on the floor. The two figures seem to ignore each other, but if we look closer we see that it is not so. It is all so obvious that it can't be explained. Even the view from above loads the scene with mystery.
As we can see from the preparatory sketches, Hopper continually changes the viewpoint like a director filming around his subject with a camera.
The painting, Hopper says, was "probably first suggested by many rides on the 'L' train in New York City after dark, [during which I caught] glimpses of office interiors that were so fleeting as to leave fresh and vivid impressions on my mind."

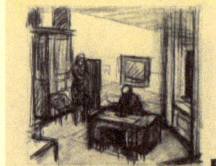

2. *Study for Office at Night*, 1940
chalk and charcoal on paper, cm 38.4x46.6
New York, Whitney Museum of American Art

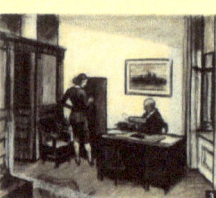

3. *Study for Office at Night*, 1940
chalk and charcoal on paper, 38.1x40.2 cm
New York, Whitney Museum of American Art

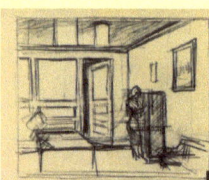

4. *Study for Office at Night*, 1940
charcoal on paper, 71.6x27.9 cm
New York, Whitney Museum of American Art

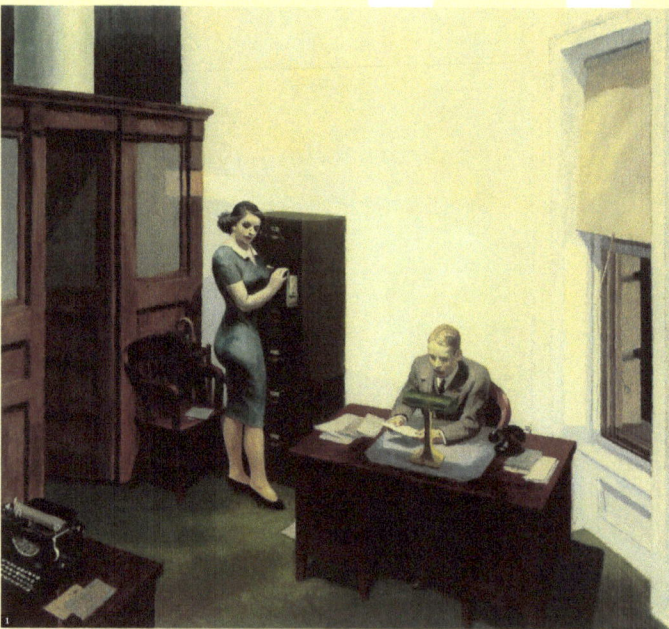

1. *Office at Night*, 1940
oil on canvas, 56.4x64 cm
Minneapolis, Collection Walker Art Center

The scene is portrayed from outside. From the pillar-framed window one sees, as if on a television screen, a woman in a tight dress reading a document.
Behind her sit two semi-hidden figures.
Despite the time of day, this place seems deserted. Hopper shows us people who do not talk to one another: each is a stranger to the other. Even the street is empty.

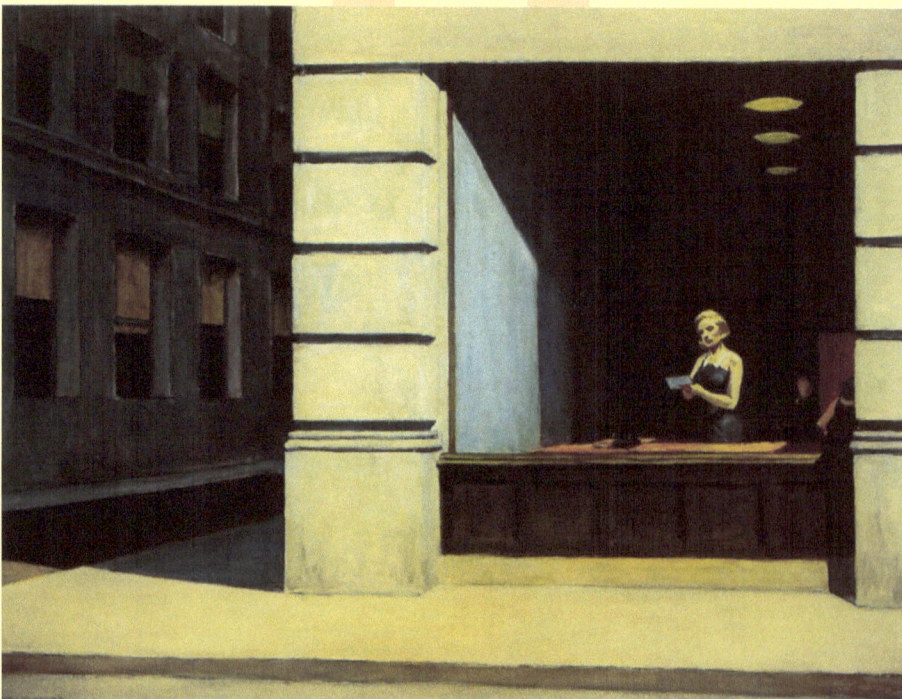

1. *New York Office*, 1962
oil on canvas, 101.6x139.7 cm
Montgomery, Museum of Fine Arts

"I must have faith," declares photographer Walker Evans. *"Otherwise I can't act. I think that what I do has a value I would call 'transcendent.' It's a heavy term to use, but I really think there is something transcendent in the pictures I took."* This *"something transcendent"* recalls the *"beyond"* found in Hopper's paintings.

1. **Dorothea Lange**, *Migrant Mother*, 1936

2. **Walker Evans**, *Gas Station*, 1935

3. **Walker Evans**, *Barber Shop, Southern Town*, 1936

4. **Walker Evans**, *Main Street Block, Selma, Alabama*, 1935

america in crisis

After World War I, the United States sees an unprecedented economic growth. This boom is followed by an equally sudden bust on Wall Street. It is the time of the Great Depression, a time that plunges thousands of Americans into misery and desperation, often to the point of suicide. Among the many initiatives designed to face the dramatic situation, President Roosevelt creates the Farm Security Administration, which was charged, among its many other functions, with documenting the situation.

With the awareness that a picture can communicate much more than words, the FSA hires many photographers, among them Walker Evans, Dorothea Lange, Ben Shahn, Arthur Rothstein, John Vachon, Jack Delano, Russell Lee, and Carl Mydans. These are artists who use their cameras not as mere means of documentation, but as instruments of expression. Many of Walker Evans' photos recall Hopper's paintings. It is not known whether the two ever met, but their works reveal a striking similarity in their artistic gazes.

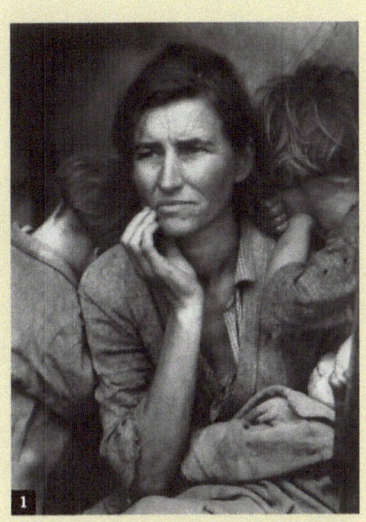

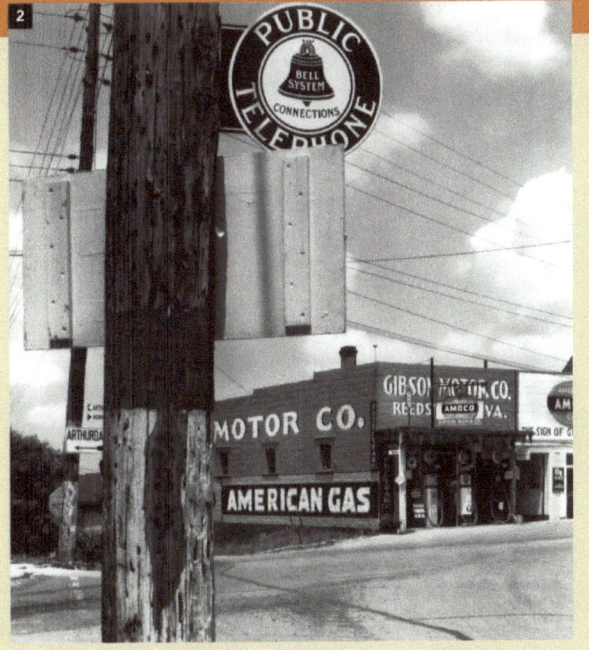

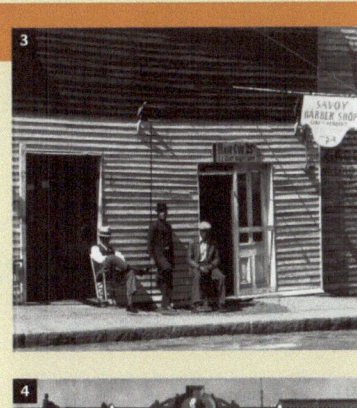

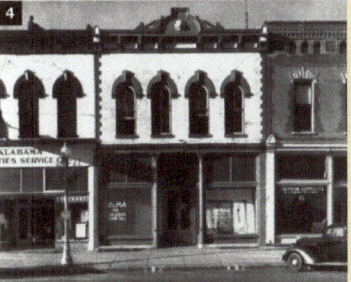

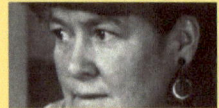

In December 1922, Hopper takes part in an exhibit at the Belmaison Gallery in New York City. Josephine Nivison (1883-1968), a student of Henri's whom Hopper had met during his training, also participates in the exhibit. In 1923, Nivison recommends that Hopper be invited to a collective at the Brooklyn Museum, where, for the first time, critics notice and praise his work. This is the moment in which Hopper can finally abandon his toilsome work as an illustrator and give himself fully to his painting.

"If I could say it in words," Hopper famously quips, "there would be no reason to paint."

a woman who becomes every woman

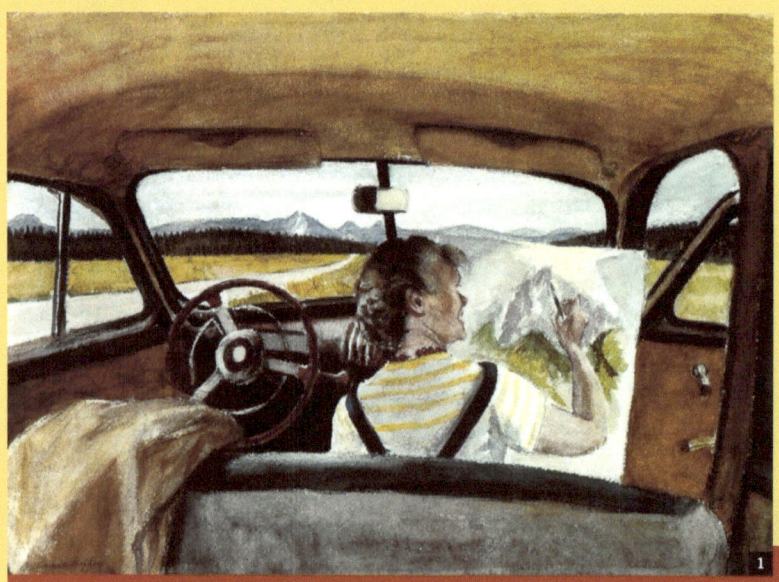
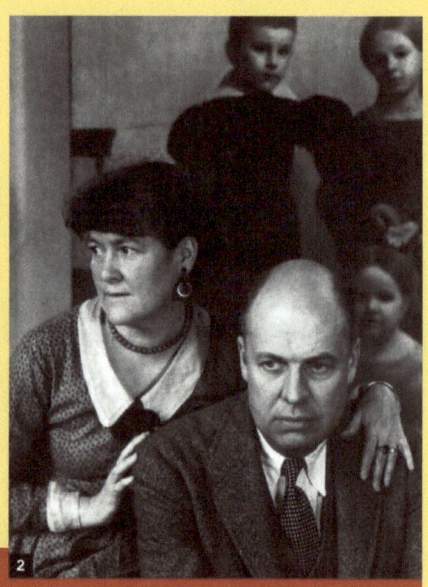

On July 9th, 1924, Edward and Jo marry at the Evangelical church on 16th Street. She will be his inseparable companion for the rest of his life. They spend their years together living in Washington Square, a place that still bore the imprint of that European tradition so loved by Hopper. Unlike Edward, who is shy, reserved, and focused on his research, Jo is lively and confident.

They had no children and lived a simple life dedicated to their painting. They split their time between the silence of Cape Cod, where they spent almost six months every year, and New York City. The female figure who appears in Hopper's paintings is almost always Jo: the woman who becomes every woman.

1. ***Jo in Wyoming***, 1946
watercolor on paper, 35.4x50.8 cm
New York, Whitney Museum of American Art

2. ***Edward and Josephine Hopper***, 1933

In 1930, Hopper visits Cape Cod for the first time.
"They bought some land in South Truro, Cape Cod, on the Massachusetts Bay: a hilly town surrounded by undulating sand, green pines and oaks. There they built a simple wooden house (the first in that area) on top of a hill overlooking the bay," wrote Lloyd Goodrich.

"I chose to live there because it has a longer summer season. There's something soft about Cape Cod that doesn't appeal to me too much. But there's a beautiful light there—very luminous—perhaps because it's so far out to sea; an island almost" (Hopper, 1962).

cape cod

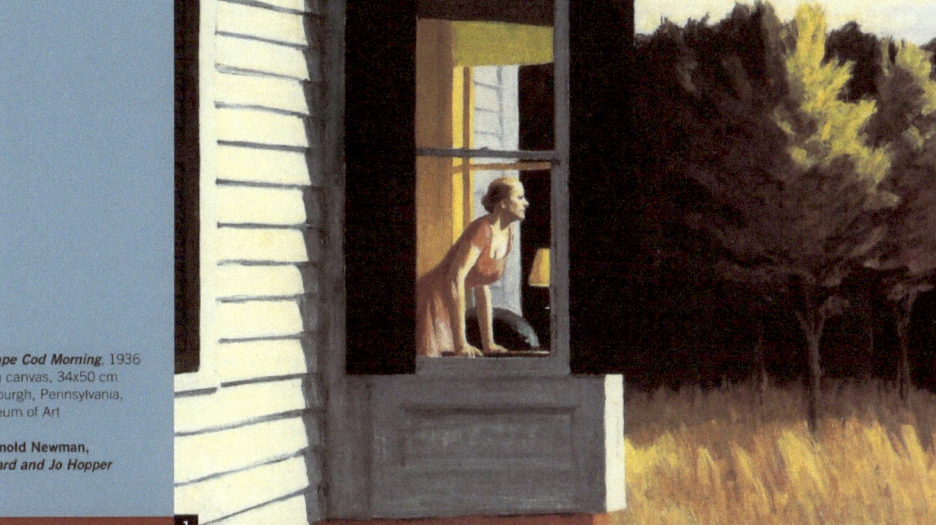

1. *Cape Cod Morning*, 1936
oil on canvas, 34x50 cm
Pittsburgh, Pennsylvania,
Museum of Art

2. **Arnold Newman,**
Edward and Jo Hopper

"When you visited them, walking along a path traced with sand between the bushes, you reached a wooden walkway and found yourself overlooking a white beach full of seagulls and surrounded only by the sea. The house, which he designed, was unadorned like his painting: in fact, those austere spaces inspired many of his works.
"From that moment, Cape Cod and its tall ocean dunes, its simple colonial homes, its wooden churches, its white villages, its salty air, became the ideal place to work. From 1930, the Hoppers spent almost half the year there and returned to Washington Square only at the end of October or November" (Lloyd Goodrich, 1971).
What attracts them is the search for a quiet and solitary life in contact with nature, despite the many practical difficulties (electricity, for example, will not arrive for another twenty years).

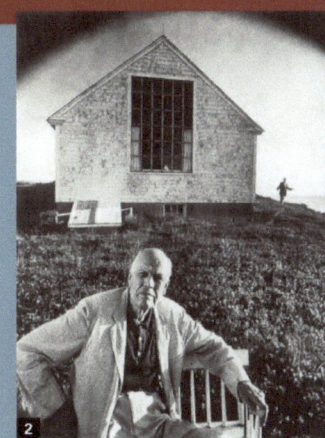

One of the recurrent themes in Hopper's works is the city. His depiction of New York, however, is not one of skyscrapers, the first automobiles, jazz, Rockefeller Center, and the Empire State Building. Hopper's New York is a solitary and deserted place. The streets are empty, and the workplaces are still, as if frozen. The spaces that are inhabited are rarely familiar: hotel rooms, offices, diners, and theaters—all spaces that people occupy but that do not belong to them.

Street corners, buildings and offices are immersed in a geometric light that freezes them in a timeless stillness. Hopper captures the most solitary and dramatic aspect of the city.

portraying the city

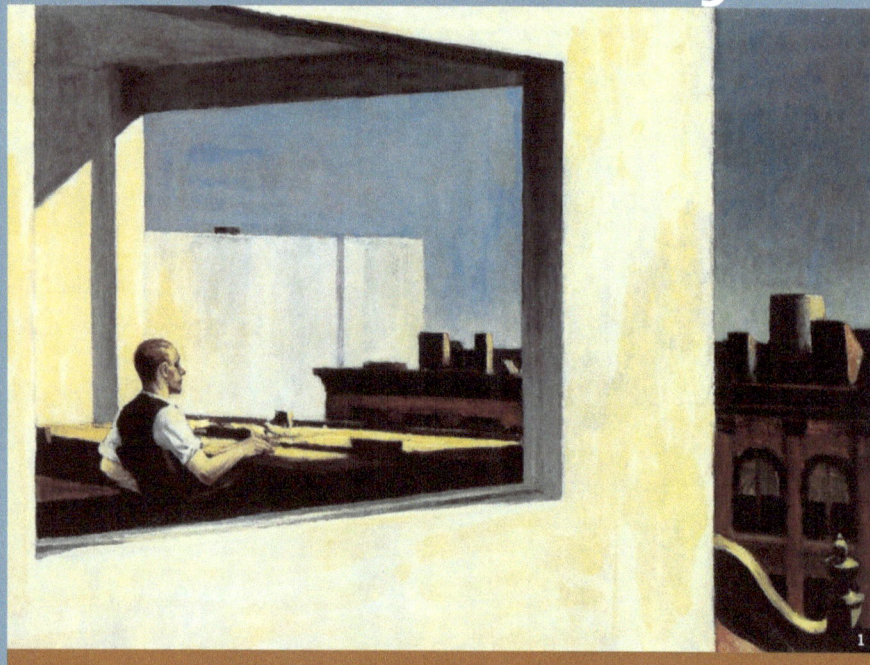

1. ***Office in a Small City***, 1953
oil on canvas, 71.7x101.6 cm
New York, The Metropolitan Museum of Art

2. ***Approaching a City***, 1946
oil on canvas, 68.9x91.4 cm
Washington, The Philips Collection

3. ***The City***, 1927
oil on canvas, 71.1x91.4 cm
Tucson, The University of Arizona Museum of Art

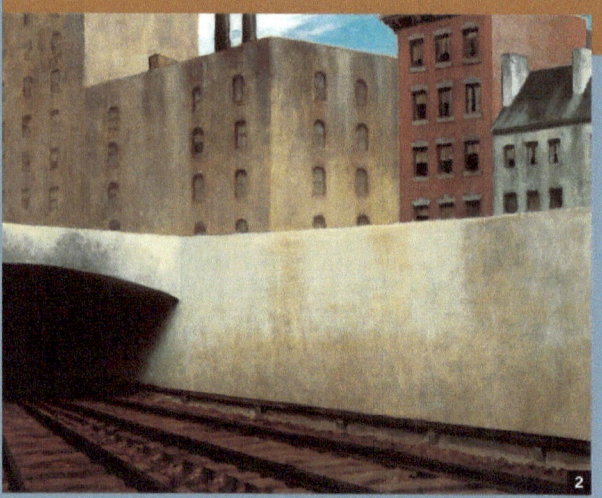

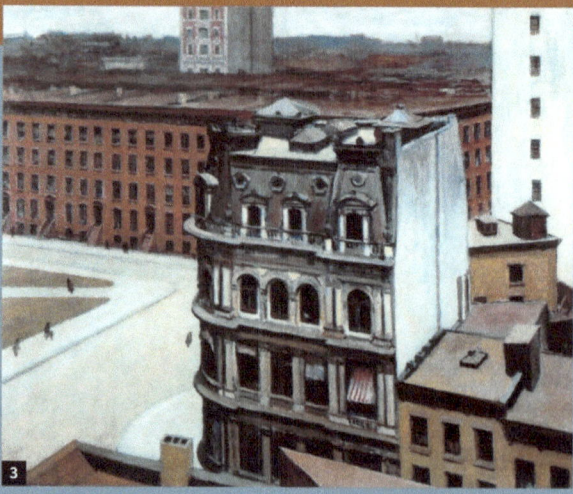

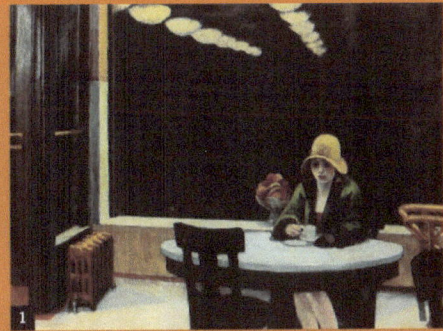

We do not know what these figures are thinking or seeing. This makes their isolation even more apparent.

solitary places

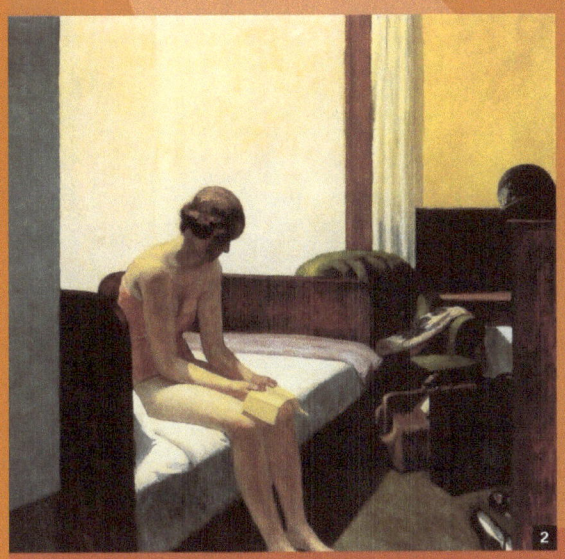

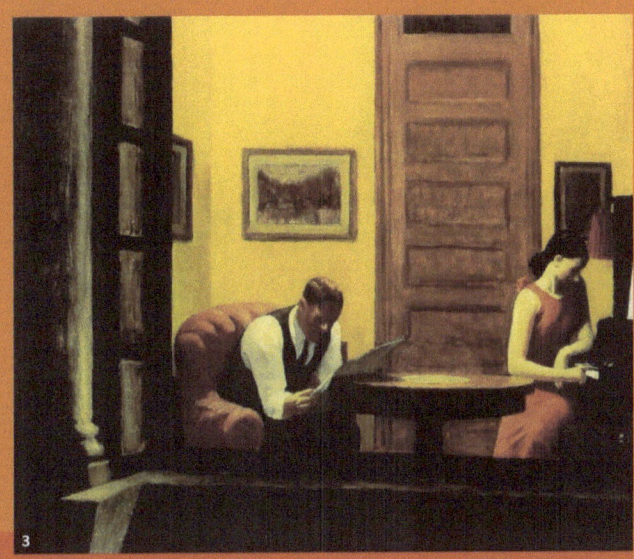

1. **Automat**, 1927
oil on canvas, 72.4x91.4 cm
Des Moines, Art Center

2. **Hotel Room**, 1931
oil on canvas,
152.4x165.7 cm
Madrid, Museo
Thyssen-Bornemisza

3. **Room in New York**, 1932
oil on canvas, 73.7x91.4 cm
Lincoln, University
of Nebraska

4. **Eleven A.M.**, 1926
oil on canvas, 71.3x91.6 cm
Washington, Hirshhorn
Museum and Sculpture
Garden

The lone subject, usually a woman, is another of Hopper's central themes. Observed in anonymous environments, in everyday moments, these figures seem to meditate on themselves and the meaning of their existence. Many of the symbols that accompany them reveal a condition of transitoriness: the coat and glove still worn (*Automat*); the luggage still on the carpet and the clothes strewn about the room (*Hotel Room*); the uncomfortable position on the stool and the finger lingering on the piano, waiting for something that might break the boredom between the two figures (*Room in New York*).

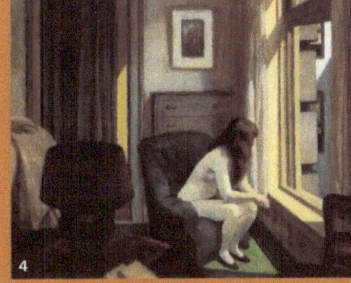

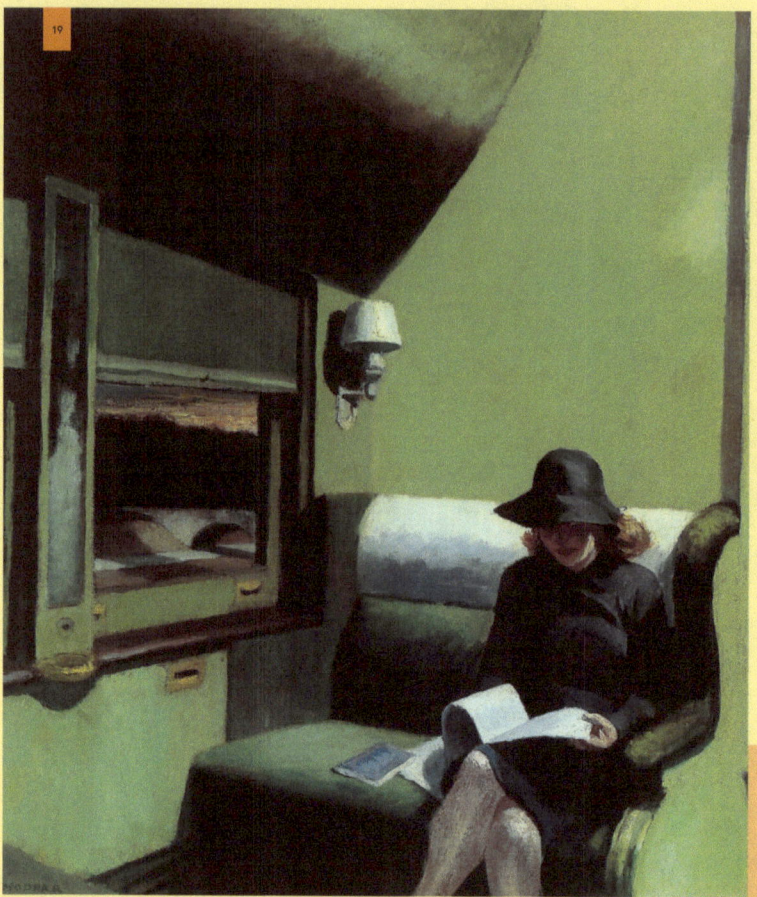

*The painting's title is reminiscent of the cold and impersonal directions on a train ticket.
The two focal points of the picture are the landscape outside and the female figure immersed in her reading. Yet the true center of this work is the emptiness.
The woman, who in a preparatory sketch looked out of the window, is now meditative.
Hopper transforms a moment in an ordinary trip into a metaphor for the human condition.*

1. **Compartment C, Car 293**, 1938
oil on canvas, 50.8x45.7 cm
New York, Collection IBM Corporation

The true subject of this painting is solitude, which every element of the composition reasserts: the deserted streets, the dark windows, the cold neon light, the man turning his back, the barman who tries a timid approach toward a client, the couple who touch one another without a look, the empty stools, the abandoned glass, the unused accessories on the bar, the dormant coffee makers. The emptiness of the outside is the same as the one in the café, but the emptiness inside is more dramatic because it is an existential fact: the emptiness of people who do not even know where to go after the establishment closes.
"Nighthawks seems to be the way I think of a night street. I didn't see it as particularly lonely. I simplified the scene a great deal and made the restaurant bigger. Unconsciously, probably, I was painting the loneliness of a large city" (Hopper, 1962).

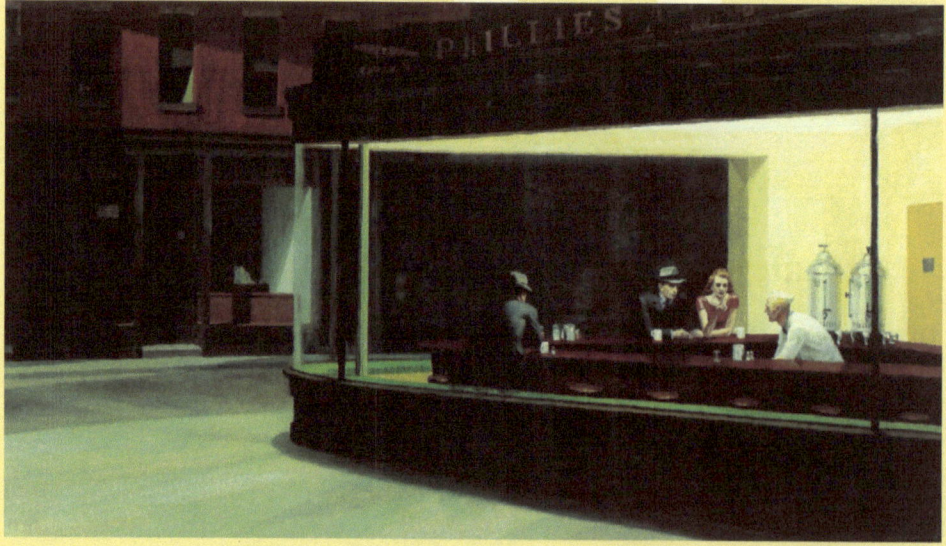

1. **Nighthawks**, 1942
oil on canvas, 76.2x144 cm
Chicago, The Art Institute

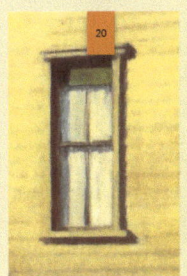

"Hopper was able to capture a specific time, almost an exact moment in which time stops, giving the instant a universal, eternal meaning," said Charles Burchfield, painter and friend of Hopper.

1. **Railroad Sunset**, 1929
oil on canvas, 71.8x121.3 cm
New York, Whitney Museum of American Art

2. **Sunday**, 1926
oil on canvas, 73.7x86.3 cm
Washington, The Phillips Collection

3. **Pennsylvania Coal Town**, 1947
oil on canvas, 71.1x101.6 cm
Youngstown, The Butler Institute of American Art

"exquisite hour"

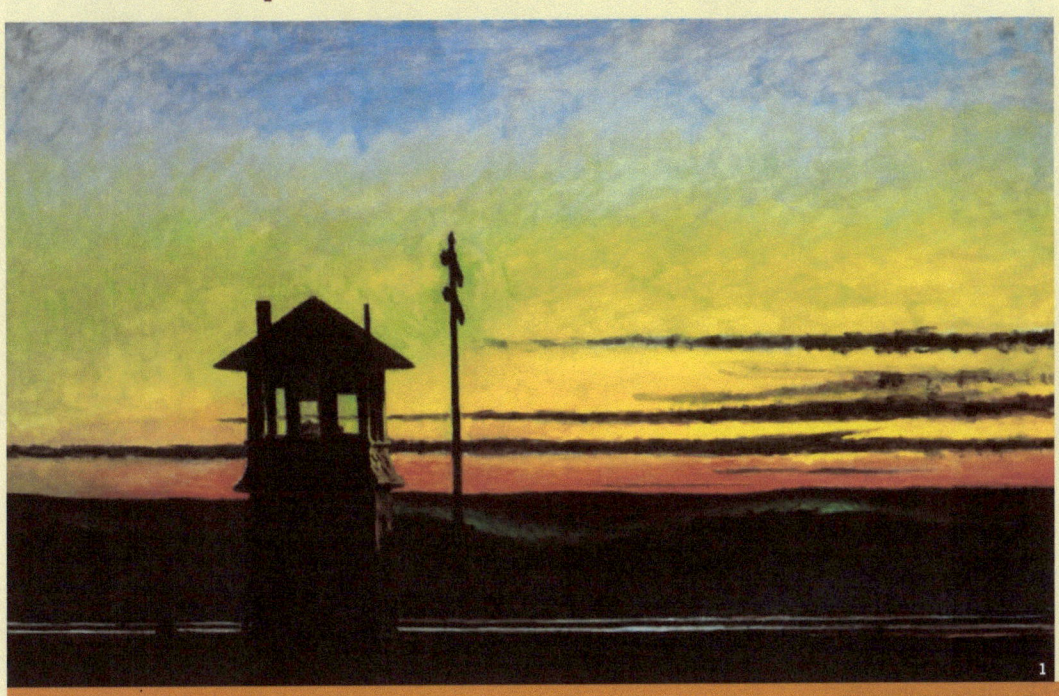

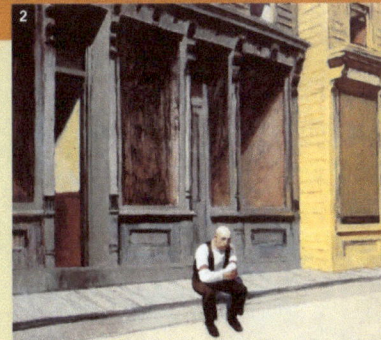

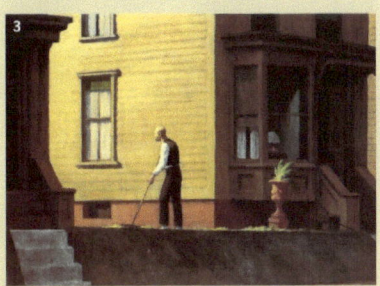

It is not by chance that Hopper loves two poems in particular—and often recites them by heart. The first is by Verlaine: "A vast and tender consolation seems to fall from the sky the moon illumines...Exquisite hour." The second is by Goethe: "Above all hilltops / it is calm. / In all tree-tops / you feel / scarcely a breath; / the birds are silent in the forest. / Only wait, soon / you, too, shall rest."

Both poems describe a suspended moment.

It is in these moments that the possibility of infinity becomes most evident, bringing with it sometimes hope, sometimes dismay at an apparent absence of meaning.

Hopper's art, which in those years had been forgotten and subsequently rediscovered by Warhol and his colleagues, is in fact quite different from Pop Art. It is not limited to the reproduction of a world in which information replaces truth. Whereas in Pop Art consuming is more important than being, Hopper expresses a constant search for meaning.

hopper and pop art

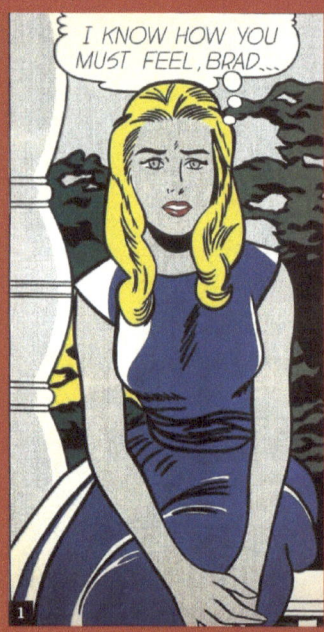

1. **Roy Lichtenstein**, *I Know How You Must Feel, Brad*, 1963, oil on canvas 168x96 cm Aachen, Neue Galerie, Sammlung Ludwig

2. **Andy Warhol**, 1985, screenprint, one of 30 copies, Lenox Board Museum

3. **Edward Ruscha**, *Standard Station, Amarillo, Texas*, 1963 oil on canvas, 165,1x308.9 cm Hanover, Hood Museum of Art

4. **George Segal**, *The Diner*, 1964-1966, plaster, wood, acrylic, formica, masonite, neon. 8.6x7.3 m Minneapolis, Walker Art Center

"What's great about this country is that America started the tradition where the richest consumers buy essentially the same things as the poorest. You can be watching TV and see Coca-Cola, and you can know that the President drinks Coke. Liz Taylor drinks Coke, and just think, you can drink Coke, too. A Coke is a Coke and no amount of money will get you a better Coke than the one the homeless man on the corner drinks. Liz Taylor knows it, the President knows it, the homeless man knows it, and you know it, too" (Andy Warhol, 1975).

In the 1950s, Pop Art is born, an artistic current bringing together Warhol, Lichtenstein, Segal, Rosenquist and others. It is inspired by mass media: cartoons, street signs, advertising, comic books. The reality in Pop Art is shown as it is, without raising questions about its meaning. This is not a criticism of society, but an ironic acceptance of what is.

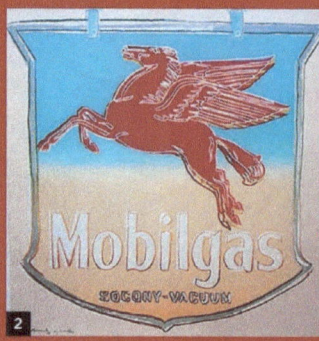

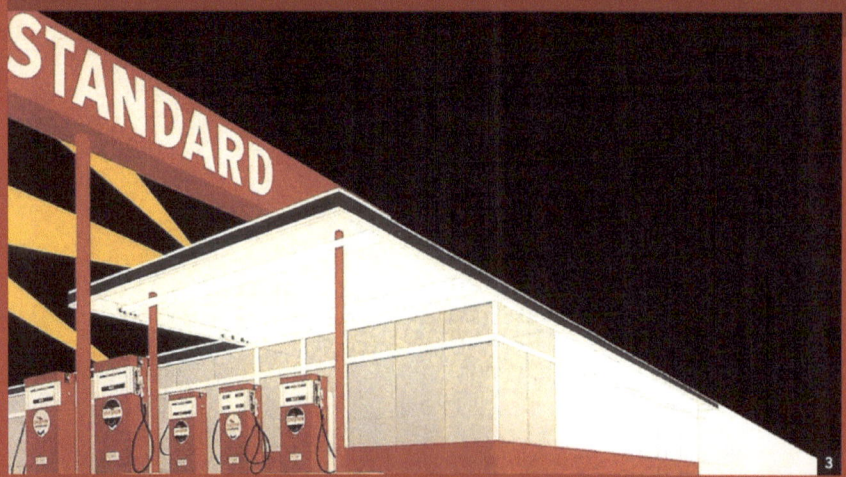

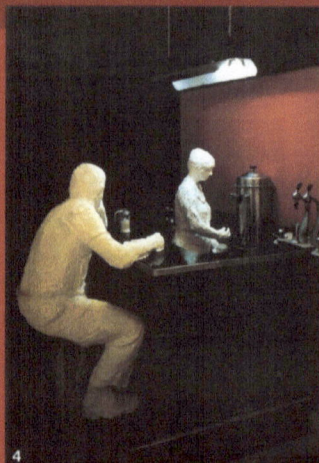

There are numerous preparatory drawings for this work, a sign of an insistent study.
Jo recounts that Hopper looked diligently for just the right gas station and, when he did not find it,
he painted it combining some sketches of real ones.
As critics have noted, here appears for the first time a "Mobil" gas station, a prelude to
Pop artworks.
The importance of this painting, however, does not depend on the brand name. In fact, it is a sort of
anti-publicity. The Mobil gas station is a painful icon of progress. In the twentieth century, human
beings invented cars, but they do not know where the path they are following leads. As a result, they
get lost in the shadowy woods. The human problem in the twentieth century is not in discovering
where to buy gas but in asking where the path leads.

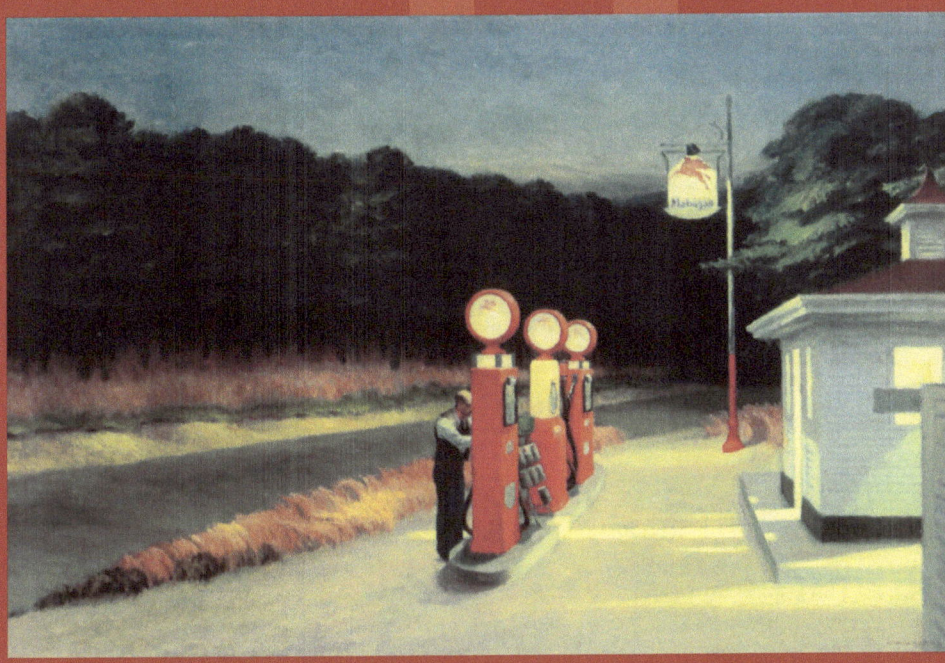

1. **Gas**, 1940
oil on canvas, 66.7x102.2 cm
New York, The Museum Of Modern Art

However, Hopper does not want to express only solitude. It would be misleading to reduce his oeuvre
to a purely psychological, subjective analysis. He himself lamented the fact that critics focused too
much on the solitude in his paintings.
Consider, for instance, a work like **Early Sunday Morning**. At first glance, this painting portrays the
sadness of a Sunday morning in which the storefronts are shuttered and the streets are empty. Yet,
as Hopper himself explains, he did not give the painting this title; it was added later.
In fact, this work does not represent the oppressive silence of non-working days, but rather an
instant in which, on an ordinary day, the city suddenly seems different, mysterious, like a metaphysical apparition.
Everything stops, and in this suspension of time what transpires is not so much a sense of solitude
as of mystery.

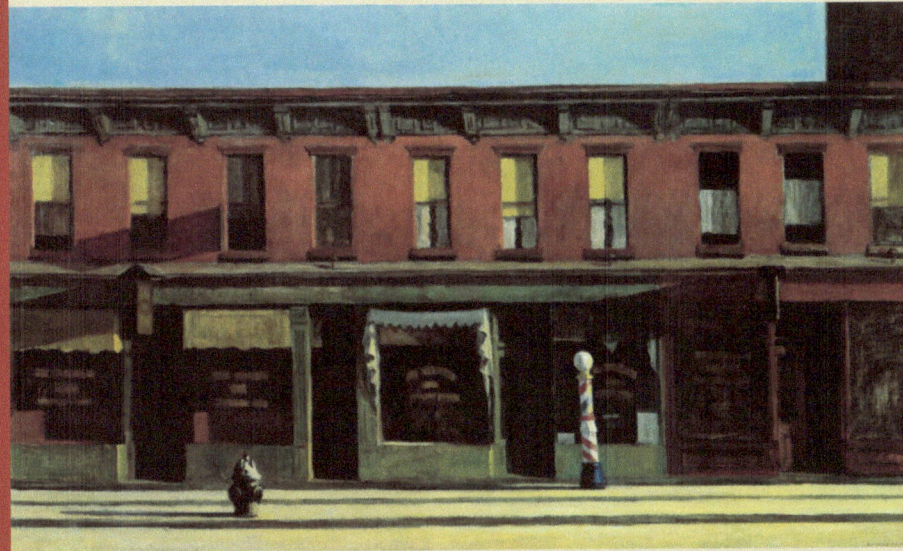

1. **Early Sunday Morning**, 1939
oil on canvas, 88.9x152.4 cm
New York, Whitney Museum of American Art

One finds a sense of expectation in many of Hopper's paintings, works in which various figures seem to turn toward an ineffable point beyond the space of the picture itself. These restless characters stand at their front door or sit by a window, clinging to a column or a banister. They are unsure of whether they should leave or stay, yet their gaze is projected forward.

1. *Summer*, 1943
oil on canvas, 74x111.8 cm
Wilmington, Delaware Art Museum

2. *Hotel Window*, 1955
oil on canvas, 101.6x139.7 cm
New York, The Forbes Magazine Collection

3. *Sunlight on Brownstones*, 1956
oil on canvas, 77.2x102.2 cm
Kansas, Wichita Art Museum

waiting for something

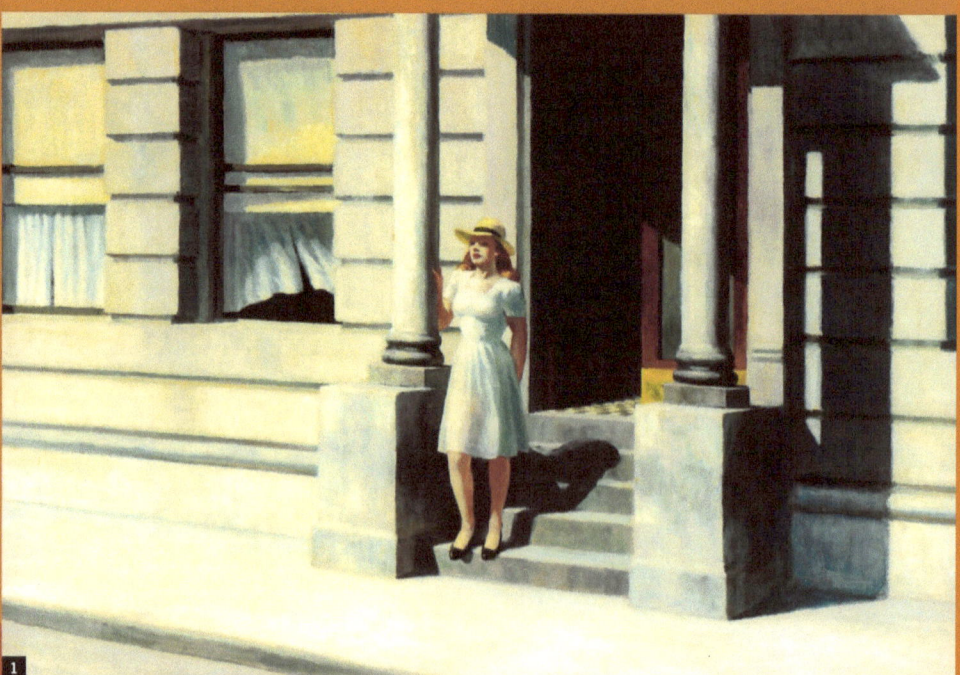

However, this awaiting is not a passive position, but is rather a tending toward something, a condition that involves the entirety of the human "I." It is within this tension that Hopper's subjects express their desire for meaning.

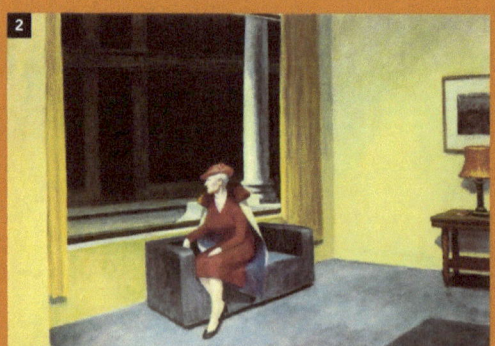
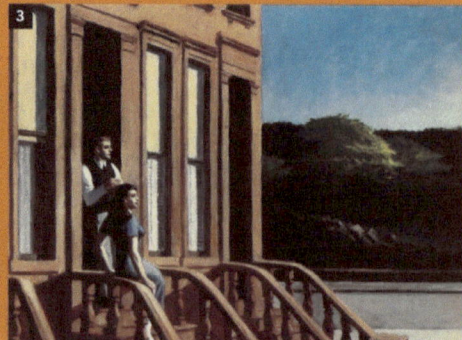

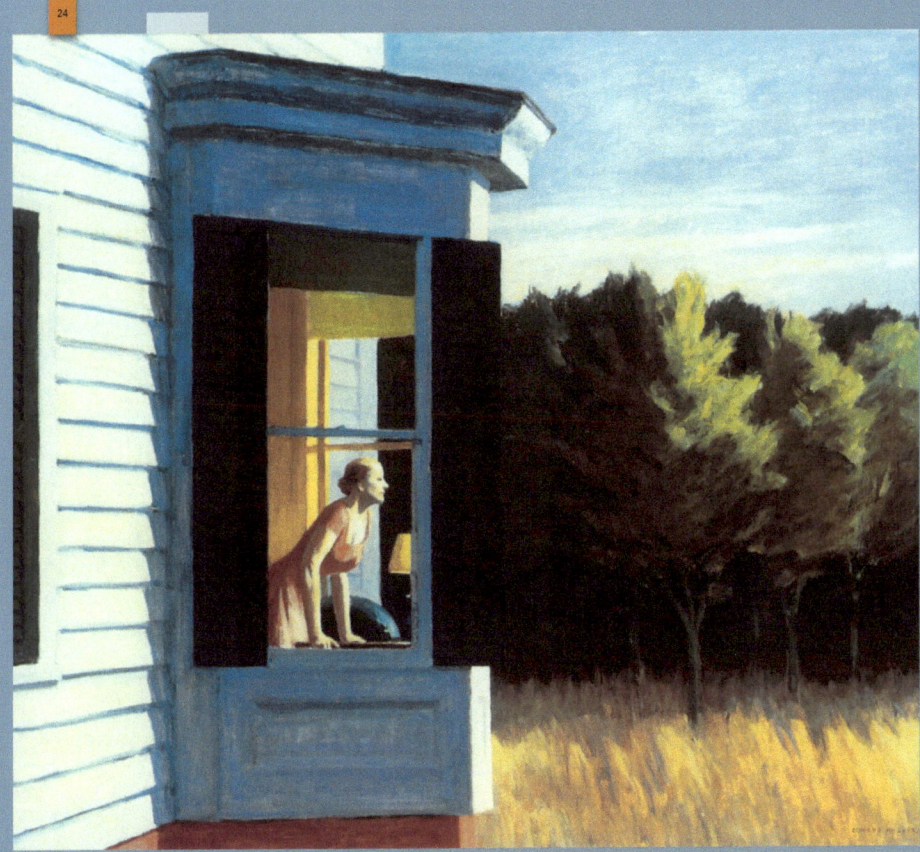

1. *Cape Cod Morning*, 1950, oil on canvas, 86.7x102.3 cm, Washington, Smithsonian American Art Museum

Hopper often depicts empty rooms. In *Rooms by the Sea*, a wall divides two empty rooms. In the first, the sun casts its light on the wall and floor. The open door gives a glimpse of sea and sky. Since the painting portrays the view of the beach in Cape Cod, one would expect to see a long stretch of sandy dunes that eventually reach the water. Yet the point of view that Hopper presents nullifies the distance between viewer and ocean, thus opening immediately onto the infinite.

"As a child I felt that the light of the high part of a house was different from that of the lower part. There is a sort of elation about sunlight on the upper part of a house."

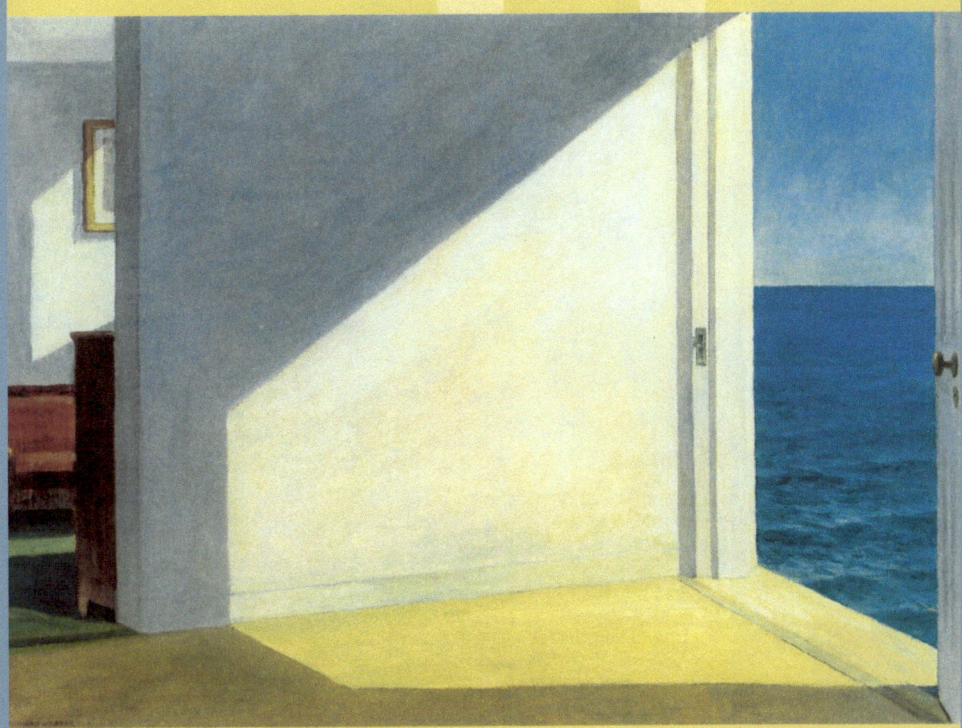

1. *Rooms by the Sea*, 1951, oil on canvas, 73x100 cm, New Haven, Connecticut, Yale University Art Gallery

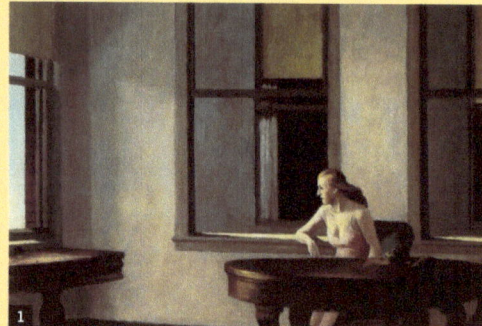

1. *City Sunlight*, 1954
oil on canvas, 71.6x101.9 cm
Washington, Hirshhorn Museum and Sculpture Garden

2. *People in the Sun*, 1960
oil on canvas, 123x153 cm
Washington, National Museum of American Art

3. *Morning in a City*, 1944
oil on canvas, 112x153 cm
Williamstown, Williams College

looking for the sun, looking for the infinite

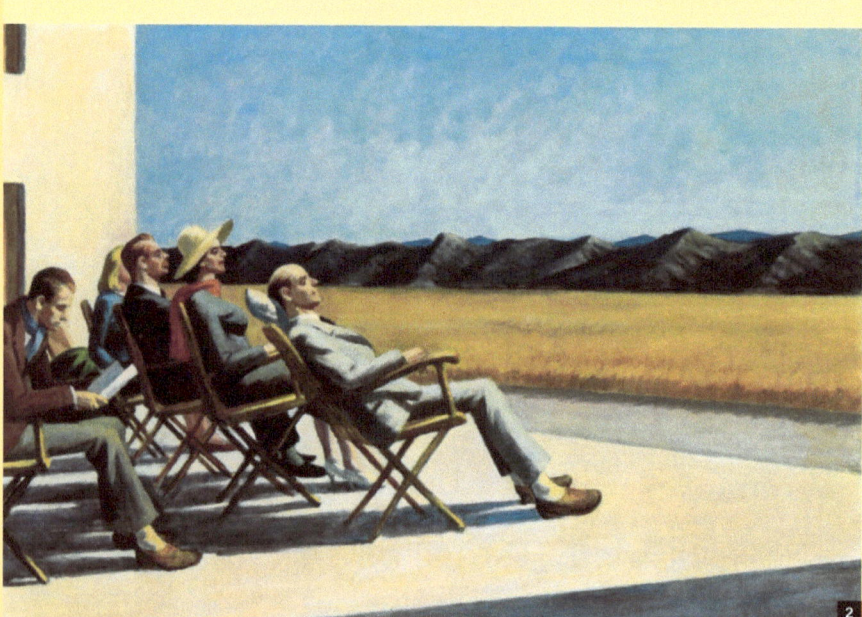

One cannot but think that the invisible sun toward which people direct their gaze, enclosed in their silence, is the mark of a metaphysical tension, of an infinite question searching for an answer.

Many of Hopper's later works feature subjects looking at the sun. It is the true protagonist of these paintings, bursting through open windows in the morning, pervading solitary rooms, illuminating the second floor of a home or the tables in a café.
Its ineluctable yet elusive presence (elusive because the white disc itself is never present), expresses the longing for, or perhaps the search for, a transcendent dimension. The utter fascination with light finally resurfaces in Hopper's last works, a fascination that, from his first visit to Paris half a century before, never diminishes.

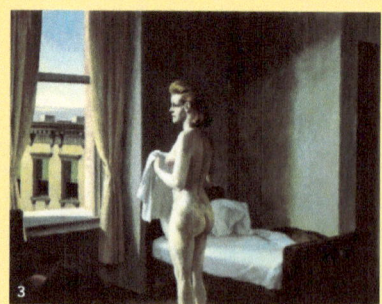

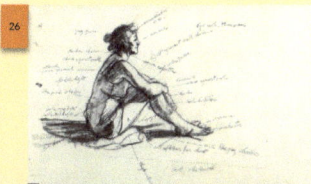

1. Study for *Morning Sun*, 1952
charcoal on paper, 30.5x48.1 cm
New York, Whitney Museum
of American Art

2. *Morning Sun*, 1952
oil on canvas, 71.4x103.9 cm
Columbus (OH),
Columbus Museum of Art

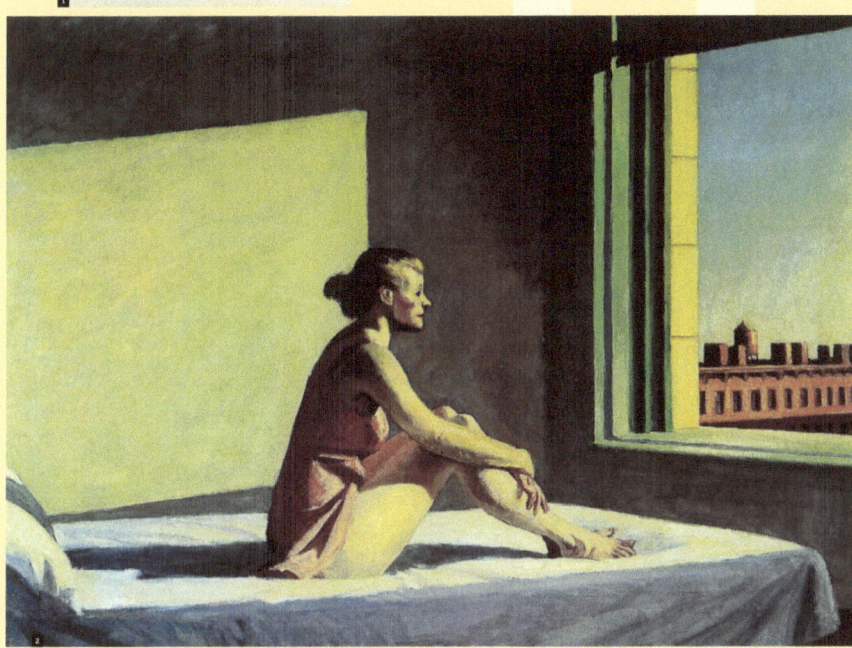

In 1965, Hopper paints two actors (himself and Jo) saluting an invisible public at the end of their last act. It is his final painting. He dies on May 15th, 1967, in his New York home. Less than a year later, Jo follows him.
This work is a spiritual testament. Not only does it express the awareness of having reached the end of the play, but it also implies that life is a great human comedy, one that art has a duty to depict.

"Painting will have to deal more fully and less obliquely with life and nature's phenomena before it can again become great," Hopper said.

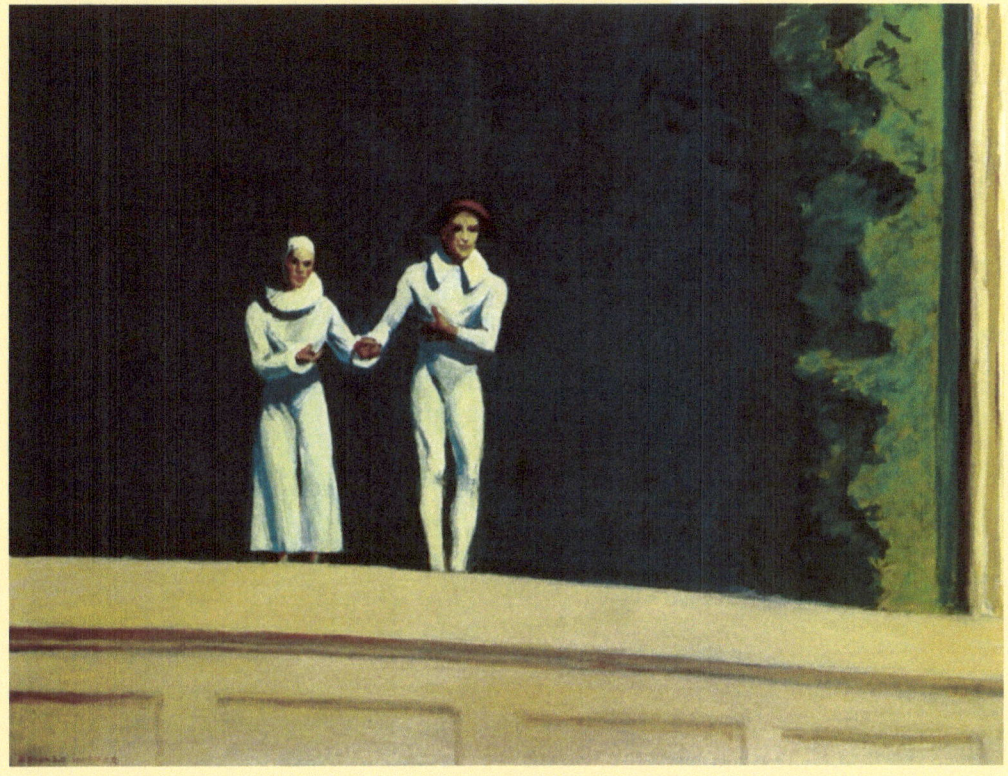

1. *Two Comedians*, 1965
oil on canvas, 73.7x100.6 cm
Private collection

www.ingramcontent.com/pod-product-compliance
Lightning Source LLC
Chambersburg PA
CBHW051833210526
45473CB00005B/1855